Discovering Our Amazing God

7th or 8th or 9th Grade Bible Curriculum

Discovering Series–Book 1

Developed and Written
by
Jan L. Harris, Howard Lisech, and Bonnie Lisech

Artwork by Bob and Mary Ann Beckett
Edited by Jaci McReynolds and Barb Snyder

additional copies may be ordered from
(see order blank at the end of this book)

Deeper Roots Publications
2100 Red Gate Rd.
Orlando, Fl. 32818
(407) 293-8666

DeeperRoots@aol.com

www.DeeperRoots.com

Student Workbook

Home School Edition

DISCOVERING OUR AMAZING GOD
Discovering Series–Book 1

Bible Curriculum for use in Grades 7, 8, & 9

HOME SCHOOL EDITION
Student Workbook ISBN 1-930547-37-4 ISBN13: 978-1-930547-37-7

Published by Deeper Roots Publications & Media
Orlando, Florida 32818

Publications available from Deeper Roots Publications www.DeeperRoots.com

Bible Curriculum Resources

ROOTED & GROUNDED – 10-12th Grade & Adult Bible Curriculum – Lisech & Harris
DISCOVERING OUR AMAZING GOD – *Book 1* 7-9th Grade Curriculum – Harris & Lisech
DISCOVERING WHO I AM IN CHRIST –*Book 2* 7-9th Grade Bible Curriculum – Harris & Lisech
DISCOVERING CHRISTLIKE HABITS –*Book 3* 7-9th Grade Bible Curriculum – Harris & Lisech
DISCOVERING CHRISTLIKE CHARACTER –*Book 4* 7-9th Grade Bible Curriculum – Harris & Lisech

Other Resources (FOR LONG & SHORT-TERM MISSIONARIES)

PRE–FIELD PREPARATION - *7 and 14 day Editions* – Howard & Bonnie Lisech
WALK AS HE WALKED - *50 day, 30 day, 21 day, and 14 day Editions* – Howard & Bonnie Lisech
ABIDE IN THE VINE - *50 day, 21 day, and 14 day Editions* – Howard & Bonnie Lisech
RIPE FOR HARVEST - *21 day, and 14 day Editions* – Howard & Bonnie Lisech
COMING HOME *Book 1* (Reentry Devotions for a Successful Return) - *14 day Overseas Return Edition* – Howard & Bonnie Lisech
COMING HOME AGAIN *Book 2* (Reentry Devotions for Another Successful Return)- 14 day *Overseas Return Edition* – Howard & Bonnie Lisech
REENTRY GUIDE FOR SHORT TERM MISSION LEADERS – Lisa Espinelli Chinn
BEFORE YOU GO - A SHORT TERM MISSIONS MANUAL – Howard Erickson

ISBN 978-1-930547-37-7
9 781930 547377 >

Table of Contents

Unreached People Profiles

Journaling

What is journaling? Journaling is simply writing your thoughts, meditations, or even prayers. Sometimes you might want to write down a great truth you have just learned.

Many times our lives are like "tumbleweeds" just rolling around, blown from one thing to another by life's pressures. Often we don't stop to think about what we are experiencing or what God is revealing to us about Himself and His will for us. You may be surprised to find that when you write your experiences down, you will understand better what God is teaching you!

I think David kept a journal. Today you can read it in the book of Psalms. He wrote, in Psa. 143:5, *I remember the days of long ago; I meditate on all your works and consider what your hands have done.* David recorded great times of joy and praise, as well as sadness and depression–times of defeat as well as victory. Today we are encouraged when we read these records of his spiritual journey.

After each lesson in your workbook, you will find pages called "Reflections." You should write your Reflections assignments on these pages, but you can also use these pages for journal entries any time you like. Your journal may not become as famous as David's. But if you take time to write thoughtfully and honestly, someday it will be an encouragement and a blessing to you.

Keeping a journal can sound intimidating, but the benefits far outweigh any inconvenience it may require. To look back and read an entry written, either during a spiritual victory or a spiritual trial, is an experience that always strengthens and encourages me.

Those day-by-day moments of learning as I walk with Jesus are too precious to be left unrecorded and forgotten. Joanna H.

I have found journaling of great importance in continually drawing my focus back to the character of God. I write letters to God and prayers about times of confession and forgiveness. I use journaling to give my burdens to Him. I write verses that remind me of His faithfulness. Linda S.

"Most of us read too much and reflect too little."
Howard Hendricks

The 10-40 Window

God's Missionary Purpose

The Bible says that God loves all people and desires that they come to know him as their Savior and Lord. *For the Son of Man has come to save what was lost.* (Luke 19:10) The Bible promises that no group will be excluded from his plan of salvation: *...because you were slain, and with your blood purchased men from every tribe and language and people and nation.* (Revelation 5:9) In God's eyes, this promise is a reality. Some day people from every group on earth will worship before His throne in heaven. *After this I looked, and there before me was a great multitude that no one could count, from every nation, tribe, people, and language standing before the throne and in front of the Lamb...* (Revelation 7:9) God's desire is that the people in the 10-40 Window will hear about Him so that His promise will be fulfilled.

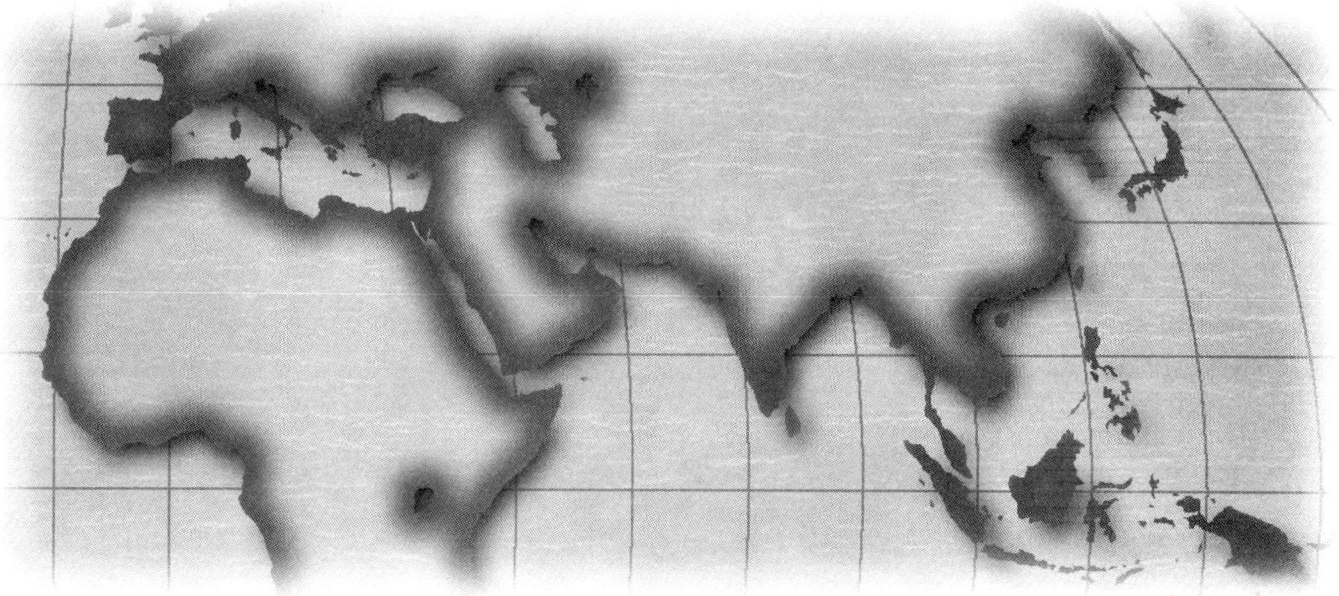

The 10-40 Window

The 10-40 Window is a term that some people use to describe a specific part of the world. It is an invisible rectangle that extends from a latitude of about 10 to 40 degrees north of the equator. Within this "window" are North Africa, the Middle East, India, Asia, and some parts of the former Soviet Union.

This region of the world is crowded with two-thirds of the world's population. Most of the poorest people in the world can be found there. They have little money for food or health care, so life expectancy is lower than in many other parts of the world.

The 10-40 Window
Continued

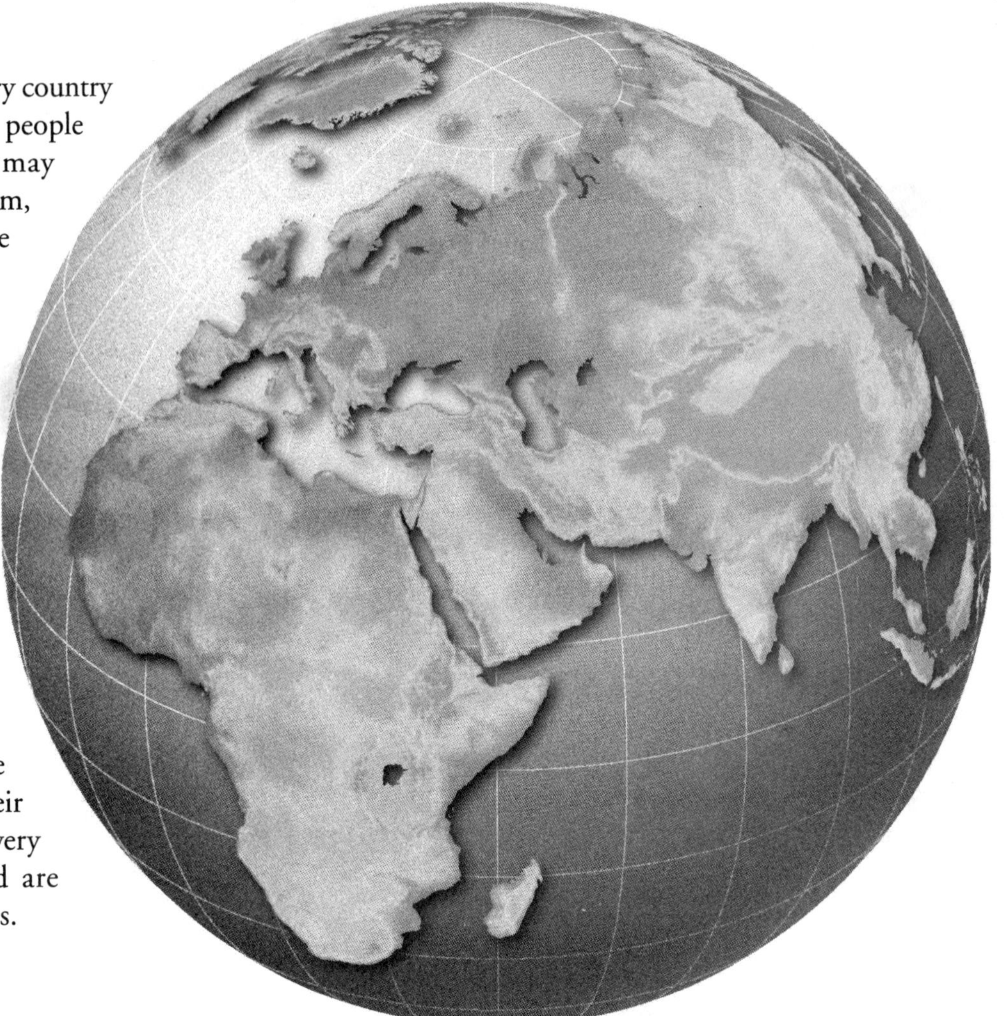

There are some Christians in every country of the 10-40 Window, but most people follow other religions. They may practice Tribal religions, Hinduism, Islam, or Buddhism. Some are atheists, believing in no God at all.

People in the 10-40 Window have little or no opportunity to learn about the true God. Many people groups there are considered "unreached." Unreached people groups have not been exposed to the gospel in a significant way. Many unreached people groups do not have Bibles in their own language. There may be no missionaries working in their area. Only one or two out of every ten missionaries in the world are working with unreached peoples.

Prayer Focus

Pray that God will raise up laborers who are willing to suffer discomfort and even danger in order to reach the people of the 10-40 window.

Sept. 7 2023

Introduction:

Discovering Our Amazing God

This is what the Lord says: "Let not the wise man boast of his wisdom or the strong man boast of his strength or the rich man boast of his riches, but let him who boasts boast about this: that he understands and knows me, that I am the Lord, who exercises kindness, justice, and righteousness on earth, for in these I delight," declares the Lord. Jer. 9:23-24

1. What does God say we should NOT boast about?

wisdom strength riches

2. What should we boast of?

we should boast about understand and know God

3. God says that when we know Him, we grow to understand and trust His character traits. Which character qualities does He list in this verse?

kindness Justice righteousness

Reflections: Spend some time thinking about what you hope to learn in Bible class this semester. Then write your thoughts in your journal.

Discovering God's Wisdom

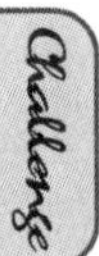

For the foolishness of God is wiser than man's wisdom, and the weakness of God is stronger than man's strength. I Cor. 1:25

Challenge

The whole Bible is a testimony of God's wisdom. In creation we see countless evidences of His wisdom. As you observe God's plans in nature, you can see His wisdom in the systems He created: the seasons, the water cycle, the seeds that reproduce plants, and the instincts he gave animals to care for their young or to migrate. The list seems endless.

> Then the Spirit of the LORD came upon me, and he told me to say: "This is what the LORD says: That is what you are saying, O house of Israel, but I know what is going through your mind." Ezek. 11:5

We see God's wisdom, too, in the lives of His people as He guides and cares for them. Think of His protection and clear guidance of Jacob, Joseph, and Moses.

God's wisdom is still evident in the lives of His children today. As we are willing to seek His plan for our lives, we can actually see His wisdom in each part of His plan.

Jesus said, "...your Father knows what you need before you ask him." Matt. 6:8b

This semester as we focus on God's attributes, or characteristics, the first attribute we will study is God's wisdom. God is not just wise– He is *all*-wise. What word means all-wise?

Discovering God's Wisdom

1. Write what you think *wisdom* means.

2. Look up *wisdom* in the dictionary and write that definition, too.

3. Do you know anyone you would consider to be truly wise? Explain your answer.

4. To the Jews, wisdom was a moral characteristic and included such things as honesty, industry, and purity. Compare the Hebrew idea of wisdom with the dictionary definition.

5. God's wisdom fits both the dictionary definition and the expanded Hebrew definition. In the Bible certain leaders were considered wise. Read the verses below and fill in the chart to show the source of their wisdom.

Reference	Person	Source of Wisdom
1 Kings 3:5-9		
Dan. 2:19-21		
Acts 6:5-10		

On Your Own: In a Bible dictionary and/or encyclopedia, look up King Ahasuerus (Xerxes) and Persia. Write a brief paragraph about each. On a map, locate the kingdom of Persia during Xerxes' reign. Be prepared to point out where Persia was located.

Day 2

1. Discuss the On Your Own assignment. Locate Xerxes' kingdom on a map.

2. Listen to the story of Esther. Try to imagine how Esther felt at each step of her journey on the path God had planned for her. When the story is finished, answer the following questions.

(a) Why did Esther live with Mordecai? (See Esther 2:5-7.)

(b) Write how you imagine Esther felt when she had to live in the palace to be trained and prepared to serve the king.

(c) Why do you think Esther was chosen to be the queen?

3. There is another story intertwined with Esther's–the story of Haman. To find out who Haman was, read Esther 3:1-6.

On Your Own: Read Esther 3:8-13 and answer the following questions.

1. What argument did Haman use to convince the king to order all the Jews killed?

2. Explain the importance of the king's ring.

3. What was Haman's real motive for killing the Jews? How do you know? Give a reference.

4. How many of the Jews did he plan to kill or have killed?

Day 3

1. How do you think Mordecai felt when he heard about the king's order? (See Esther 4:1-3.)

2. It is interesting to see that in God's wisdom, He already had a plan in place to save His people. Read Esther 4:4-9. What do you think God's plan was?

3. Read Esther 4:10-12. How do you think Esther felt about God's plan? Explain.

4. Read Esther 4:12-17. Which verse shows you that Mordecai believed God had a plan in place all along?

On Your Own: God's word says in Prov. 21:1, "The king's heart is in the hand of the Lord; He directs it like a watercourse wherever He pleases." In the sixth chapter of Esther, God has an ironic twist in His plan. Read 6:1-10 and answer these questions.

1. Who do you think caused the king's sleeplessness?

2. Who gave the king the idea to have the book of records read to him?

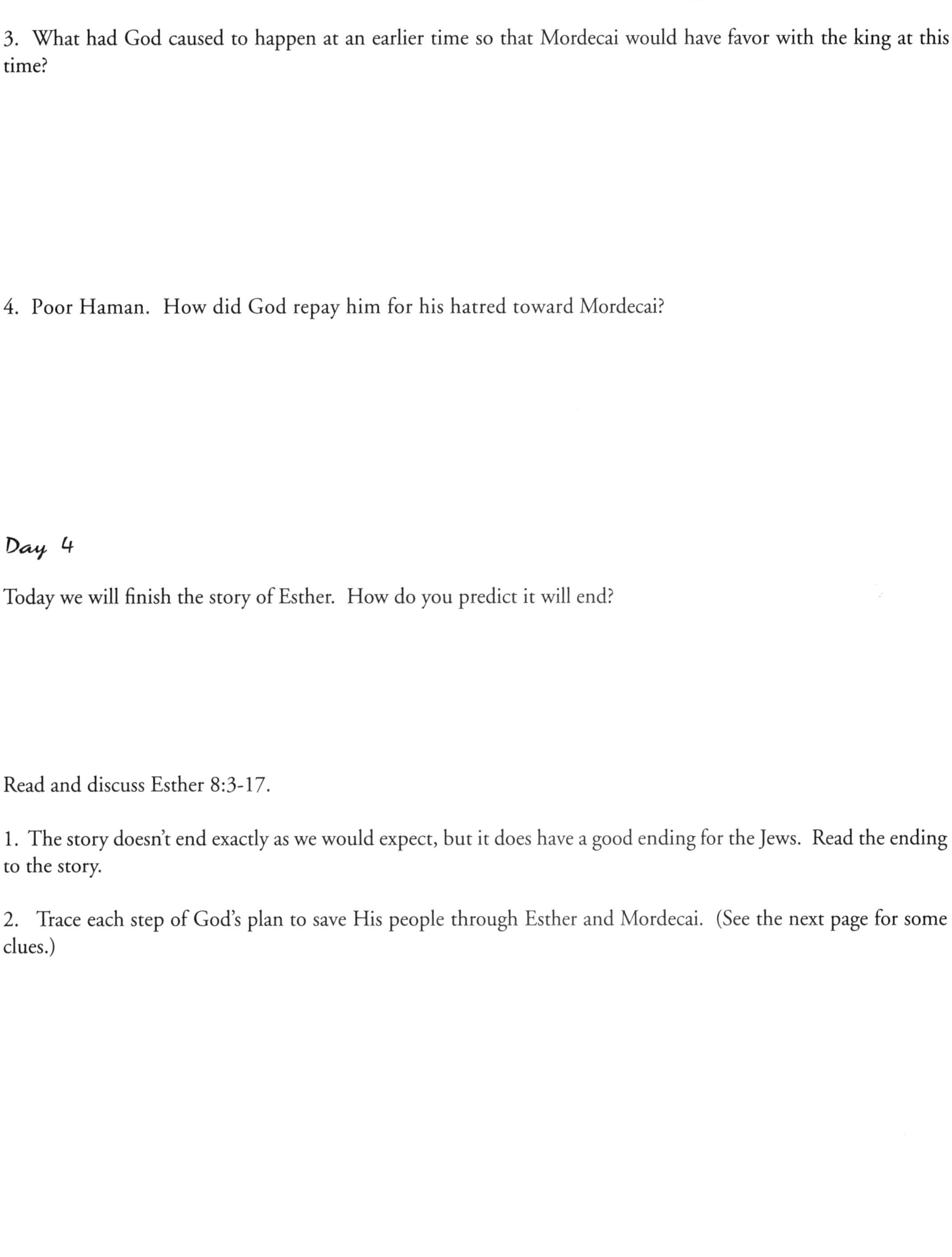

3. What had God caused to happen at an earlier time so that Mordecai would have favor with the king at this time?

4. Poor Haman. How did God repay him for his hatred toward Mordecai?

Day 4

Today we will finish the story of Esther. How do you predict it will end?

Read and discuss Esther 8:3-17.

1. The story doesn't end exactly as we would expect, but it does have a good ending for the Jews. Read the ending to the story.

2. Trace each step of God's plan to save His people through Esther and Mordecai. (See the next page for some clues.)

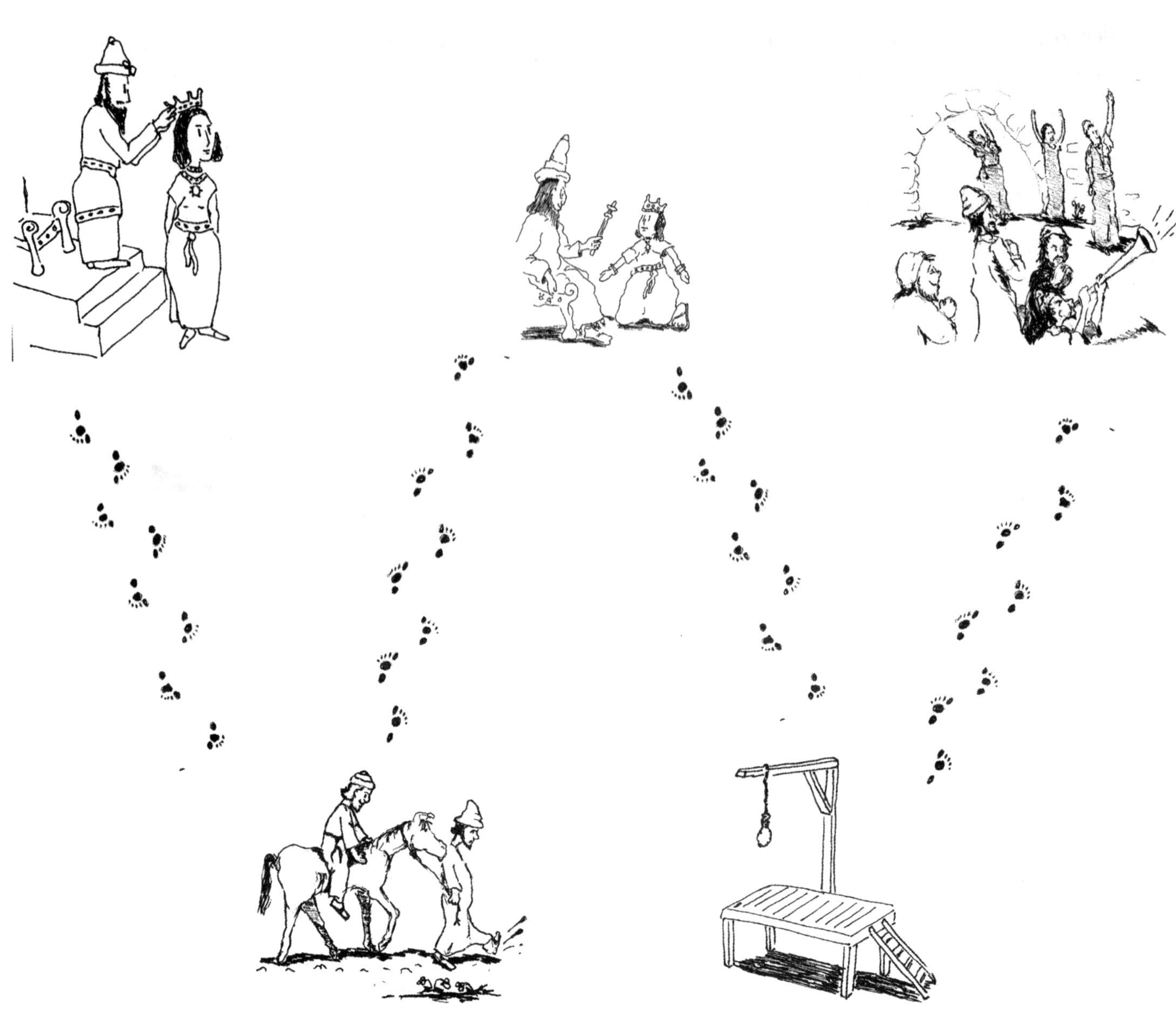

3. List three evidences of God's wisdom from the story of Esther.

4. If God could plan the circumstances of Esther's life, do you think He also has a plan for you?

Reflections: Think about your own life. In your journal, write a paragraph describing how you see God's wisdom at work in your life.

Remember, your memory challenge is due tomorrow.

Day 5

1. Write or recite your memory challenge for a grade.

2. Today we will have a guest speaker who will share with us some evidences of God's wisdom worked out in his/her life.

Day 6

Memory Challenge

Oh, the depth of the riches of the wisdom and knowledge of God! How unsearchable his judgments, and his paths beyond tracing out! Romans 11:33

Writing opportunity!

Proverbs is an entire book of the Bible devoted to some of God's wisdom. Read the following proverbs. Choose the one you like best and write a creative story which illustrates the wisdom of the proverb. You may use a true story or fiction. You will have class and On Your Own time today and tomorrow to finish your story, so you should be able to do a good job. When you come to class tomorrow, you should have at least half of your rough draft finished.

Choose from the following Proverbs:

Prov. 3:5-6 *Trust in the LORD with all your heart and lean not on your own understanding; in all your ways acknowledge him, and he will make your paths straight.*

Prov. 15:1 *A gentle answer turns away wrath, but a harsh word stirs up anger.*

Prov. 16:18-19 *Pride goes before destruction, a haughty spirit before a fall. Better to be lowly in spirit and among the oppressed than to share plunder with the proud.*

Prov. 18:13 *He who answers before listening–that is his folly and his shame.*

On Your Own: Work on your story. Have at least half of your rough draft finished by tomorrow.

WRITING SCOREBOARD

1. Content: Does the story illustrate the proverb? (60%)

2. Creativity: Is this clearly your own story? It may be a true story from your family or your own experience, but it should not be something you read or saw on TV. (10%)

3. Reality: Do the characters act and sound like real people? (10%)

4. Organization: Does the story follow a logical pattern? (10%)

5. Mechanics: Grammar, spelling, etc. (10%)

Day 7

Work on your story in class.

On Your Own: Work on your story. It is due tomorrow.

Day 8

1. Since Jesus is also God, we would expect Him to also be filled with wisdom. Can you think of anything Jesus did that you consider particularly wise?

2. Do you remember the story of Jesus teaching in the temple when He was only twelve? Retell that story. (Luke 2:43-47)

3. Jesus is wise in all His ways. He taught with parables, He used illustrations the people could relate to, and He understood their thoughts and motives. He was always able to respond in the wisest way.

Toward the end of Jesus' ministry, the Sadducees and Pharisees tried to trick Jesus into saying something that would discredit Him with the people or with the Roman government. Jesus was so wise that He was able to avoid their traps and turn the tables to put them on the defensive.

4. Read Luke 20:20-26

(a) The Chief Priests sent spies to ask Jesus questions because they wanted to____________________________

____.

(b) We know Jesus was aware of their purpose because Luke wrote, ____________________________________

____.

(c) Give a reference for (b).

(d) At the end of this question-answer period, the spies felt ______________________________

____

because____.

On Your Own: The next trick question came from the Sadducees. They asked, *If a woman's husbands keep dying until she has had altogether seven husbands, which one of the men will be her husband after the resurrection?*

Read Jesus' answer in Luke 20:34-38.

1. Summarize His answer briefly.

2. What did the scribes and Sadducees think about this answer? How do you know?

3. What do Jesus' answers to the learned religious people of His day tell you about Him?

4. Jesus could see into the hearts of the scribes and Pharisees. How does that relate to your life?

Day 9

It is actually impossible to dissect the characteristics of God. When we see Him acting in power, He is also acting in wisdom. When He is creating something, His wisdom and power are both being used. Our problem is that God's wisdom is so far above us, that we cannot grasp it. Humans are just now unscrambling the secrets of the atom and DNA. These are things God created! Our minds are so limited, we can't even imagine what else is in our universe that we haven't discovered yet!

Work on your study sheet.

On Your Own: Study for a test over Lesson 1.

Day 10

Read or recite the memory challenges. Take a test.

Lesson 1–Study Sheet

1. Define wisdom.

2. God says that in comparison to His wisdom, man's wisdom is ______________________________.

3. List three Bible characters known for their wisdom.

4. Name and briefly describe the five main characters in the book of Esther.

5. Esther lived in the kingdom of ______________________.

6. Haman hated Mordecai because ____.

7. Put the following events from the book of Esther in chronological order.
   (a) The enemy of the Jews is hanged.
   (b) Esther becomes Queen.
   (c) The king honors Esther's cousin.
   (d) The king divorces his current Queen.
   (e) Esther's cousin saves the king's life.
   (f) Esther gives a banquet for the king.
   (g) The enemy of the Jews plots against them.

8. Write or paraphrase three verses from Proverbs which we read in class. Be prepared to explain what each one means.

9. Write one of the questions the Jewish religious leaders used to try to trick Jesus. Give His answer.

Reflections

Reflections

Reflections

Reflections

Reflections

Reflections

The Muslim People

Image courtesy of PIONEERS

At one time, we thought Muslims only lived in the Middle East. It is true that Islam began in Saudi Arabia and spread quickly to neighboring countries: Iraq, Iran, Syria, Egypt, etc. However, today there are over one billion Muslims in the world, and Islam is practiced not just in the Middle East, but in countless other countries.

The Muslim People
continued

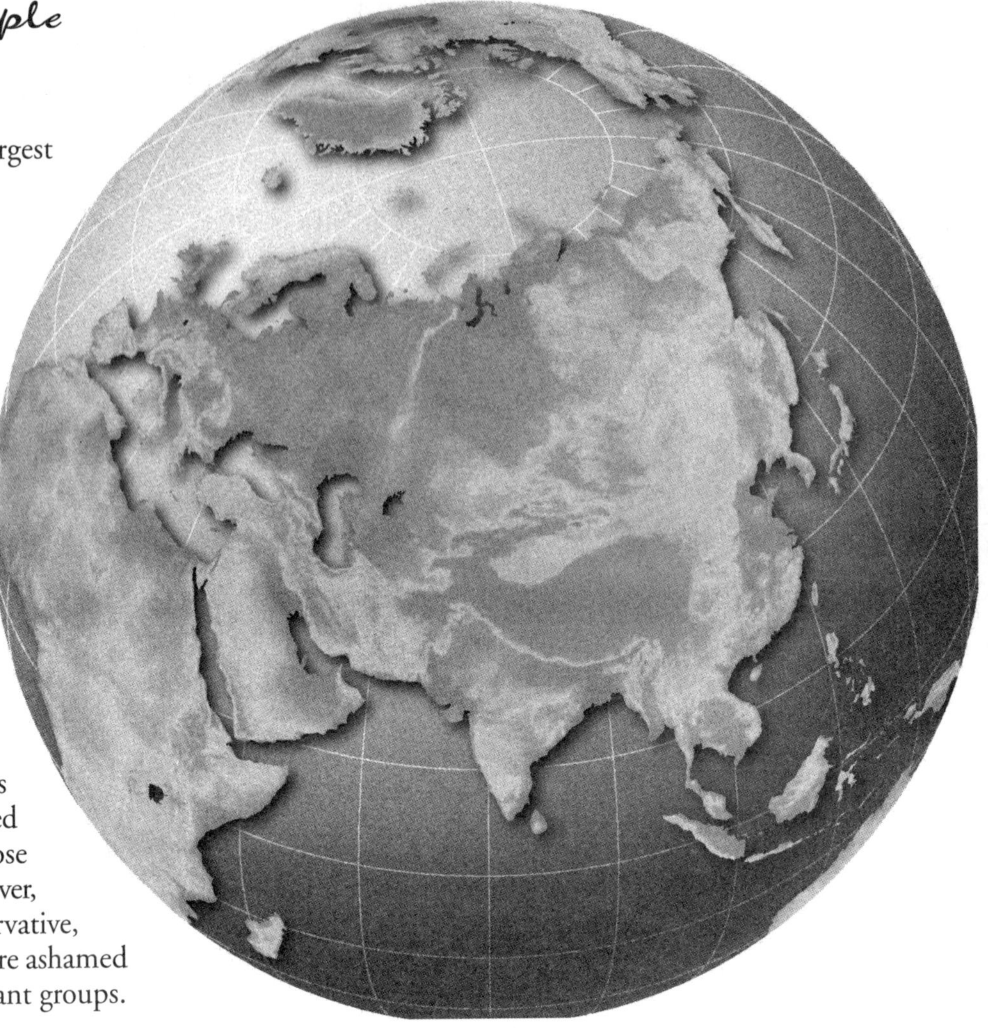

Indonesia, for example, has the largest Muslim population in the world.

The Islamic religion was started by Muhammad about 610 AD. He declared that he received special messages from God (Allah) delivered to him by Gabriel. He wrote these teachings in a holy book–the Koran. Muhammad did believe that Jesus was a prophet of God, but He was a lesser prophet than Muhammad. Today some Muslims teach their children that followers of Jesus are evil and to be avoided.

There are militant sects of Muslims who are filled with hatred and trained to inflict terror and damage on those who do not believe as they do. However, many Muslims are peaceful, conservative, honest, hardworking people who are ashamed of the evil deeds of the more militant groups.

Nearly all followers of the Muslim faith are surrounded by restrictive laws. Women must wear long sleeves and long skirts or pants and keep their heads covered. Everyone prays five times a day. There are required fasts, almsgiving, and witnessing. All these rules do not solve their sin problem. The Muslim people have an emptiness in their hearts that only Christ can fill. Personal relationship and trust are the keys to sharing the message of Christ as Savior with a Muslim friend. Why should they listen unless they know and trust the one who is sharing the message of hope?

Prayer Focus

For Christians to be willing to live sacrificially to take the gospel to Muslims.

For God to work in the hearts of Muslims to draw them to Himself.

For Christians in the United States to reach out to their Muslim neighbors with love and kindness in order to earn the opportunity to share Christ with them.

For safety for those who live intentionally in areas of the world where the Muslim religion is dominant.

Discovering God's Power

Memory Challenge

Do not be terrified by them, for the LORD your God, who is among you, is a great and awesome God. **Deut. 7:21**

To God belong wisdom and power; counsel and understanding are His. Job 12:13

Did you ever wish you could be like Superman–faster than a speeding bullet, able to leap tall buildings in a single bound? From Superman to Pokemon to Harry Potter, our culture has always been fascinated with power. Books, movies and TV often portray characters with supernatural power. In real life, people gain power over others with money, beauty or manipulation. Did you know you can buy books that teach you how to manipulate your friends and enemies? Why? So you can have "the power."

1. Who is the most powerful person you know?

2. God is powerful. God is *all*-powerful. What is the word we sometimes use to describe God that means all powerful?

3. Read the following verses to learn some of the areas that are under God's power.

Reference:	God has power over:
(a) Ps. 33:6-9	
(b) Dan. 4:35	
(c) James 4:12-15	
(d) Job 1:12 and 2:6	
(e) Eph. 1:19-21	

4. Of all the Bible stories you know, which one do you think best demonstrates God's power? This is a hard choice, so after we talk about several, you may want to change your vote.

It's interesting to see that all through the Old Testament the Hebrews would remind themselves of their deliverance from Egypt, including the plagues and the crossing of the Red Sea. Stephen even recalled these miracles in his sermon to the Jews right before he was stoned (Acts 7:36). This was clearly a great manifestation of God's power to the Jews.

In this lesson, we'll study two stories that demonstrate God's power–one from the Old Testament and one from the New Testament. At the end of the lesson, you'll have an opportunity to choose again the story that you believe best portrays God's power and to write a short paper about it.

5. Since we know that God created and controls the universe, we can also see evidence of God's power all around us. What can you think of in nature that displays God's power?

On Your Own: Read Rom. 1:18-20 and write the answers to the following questions.

1. How does God feel about wicked men?

2. According to Paul, why is He right to feel this way?

3. How has God shown His eternal power to man?

4. If a man denies the existence of God, does he have an excuse? Explain why or why not.

Day 2

1. Read Rom. 1:18-20. Go over your On Your Own assignment in class.

2. Watch a video and discuss how it shows God's power.

Writing Opportunity!

You will have the next four days to research and write a report on one of the following events which shows God's power in nature.

(1) The eruption of Krakatoa in 1883;

(2) the New Madrid earthquakes of 1811-1812;

(3) the tsunami in Papua New Guinea in 1998;

(4) the tri-state tornado in 1925;

(5) Hurricane Andrew in 1992.

- Day 1: Bring in a list of some sources and notes you have taken from each one.
- Day 2: Bring in either additional notes or a rough draft.
- Day 3: Rough draft is due. (Note: Your rough draft should be double spaced so you have room to make needed changes.)
- Day 4: Final draft is due.

GUIDELINES FOR REPORT

1. The report should be at least one handwritten page or one-half a typed page long.

2. You are required to use two to four sources. At the end of the report, you should include a list of all the sources you used.

3. You may include pictures for extra credit.

WRITING SCOREBOARD

1. Content: Is the information accurate and complete? (70%)

2. Organization: Do the paragraphs have topic sentences? (10%)

3. Following directions: Is the report two paragraphs long? Does it include a list of two to four sources? (10%)

4. Mechanics: Grammar, spelling, etc. (10%)

5. You may earn extra points for using more than two sources and for adding pictures.

Day 3

Ahab son of Omri did more evil in the eyes of the LORD than any of those before him. **1 Kings 16:30.**

In 874 BC, 56 years after the death of Solomon, Ahab became King of Israel. The Bible describes Ahab as the king who "did more evil in the eyes of the LORD than any of those before Him."

What did Ahab do that was so bad? Keep reading to find out.

- He took a wife who was not an Israelite–something strictly forbidden by God's law.
- He built altars to Baal and Asherah and worshipped them, and he encouraged the Israelites to worship both Baal and Asherah as well.
- He tried to kill Elijah. He imprisoned the prophet Micaiah.
- He was so wicked that even today his name is a symbol of a wicked king.

God told Elijah to warn Ahab that God was sending a drought. God stopped the rain in Israel for three years. During the third year of drought, God sent Elijah to confront Ahab once again.

1. Read I Kings 18:1-25.

2. Who was Obadiah?

3. What request did Elijah make of Obadiah?

4. Obadiah did not want to undertake this errand for Elijah because ____

____.

5. Elijah reassured Obadiah that he did indeed want to talk to Ahab. When Ahab saw Elijah, what did he call Elijah?

6. Elijah wanted Ahab to meet him at ______________________________ with

______________________________ .

7. Elijah was about to test the prophets of Baal. Using I Kings 18:20-24, draw a picture in each box to represent the four events Elijah had planned. Write the verse number under each box.

v. ______________ v. ______________

v. ______________ v. ______________

8. Which event would prove whether God or Baal was real?

9. What did the Israelites who were watching say about Elijah's plan? (v. 24)

10. Discuss your answers and check your work.

On Your Own: Tomorrow you should show additional notes of research and/or a rough draft of your report. Review your memory challenge. It will be graded in two days.

Day 4

Briefly review the story begun yesterday. How do you think this story will end?

1. Read I Kings 18:26-40.

2. After the prophets of Baal called on him from __________________until ____________________, Elijah began to taunt them.

(a) What does *taunt* mean? (Look it up if you need to.)

(b) List three things Elijah said to taunt the prophets of Baal.

3. How long did the prophets spend trying to get Baal to send fire for the sacrifice?

4. Draw a sketch of the altar that Elijah built. Include all the details from verses 31-33.

5. How many jars of water did the people pour on the sacrifice?

6. Why do you think Elijah told the people to do this?

7. The false prophets spent all day crying out to Baal. In contrast, Elijah spent ______________________ calling out.

8. List all five things God's fire burned up.

9. How did the people react to this demonstration?

10. Why did they react this way?

Reflections: (1) Close your eyes and try to picture fire falling from Heaven and consuming even the stones, the water, and the damp earth. Write a few sentences in your journal telling how you feel about God's demonstration of power in this story.

(2) The Bible says, "Come and see what God has done, how awesome his works in man's behalf." Ps. 66:5. Write a few more sentences explaining how this knowledge encourages you.

On Your Own: Remember, the rough draft of your report is due tomorrow. Also, your memory challenge will be graded tomorrow.

Day 5

1. Write or recite the memory challenge for a grade.

2. From Ahab's anger to the final awe of the Israelites, this is a story filled with emotion. Choose a part in this story that you can act out. Re-read your part and think about what you can do to show the emotions of your role. Act this story out in class. Try to imagine how you would feel if you had been present. At the end of your drama, pretend to be an Israelite and act as they did in v. 39.

On Your Own: Your report is due tomorrow.

Day 6

Memory Challenge

Jesus said to her, "I am the resurrection and the life. He who believes in me will live, even though he dies; and whoever lives and believes in me will never die. Do you believe this?" John 11:25–26

1. Share your report with your teacher.

2. Last week we read an Old Testament account that demonstrated God's power. Would you expect to see the same demonstrations of power in the New Testament? Why or why not?

3. There is no fire falling from heaven in the New Testament. There is nothing comparable to the crossing of the Red Sea or the destruction of the walls of Jericho, but Jesus did demonstrate His power to the people around Him. Take a minute to think quietly about some of His powerful acts. When you are ready, get out a blank sheet of paper.

In three minutes write as many evidences of Christ's power in the New Testament as you can.

4. Compare your list to your teacher's list. Did you think of the same things?

5. Using information found in John 10:40 and John 11:1 and 17, take a red pencil and indicate Jesus' trip to the home of Lazarus on the map on the next page. Use the altitude key to estimate how long it took Jesus and his disciples to make the trip.

On Your Own: Read John 11:1-15 and answer the following questions.

1. Why did the sisters send word to Jesus about Lazarus' illness?

2. How long did Jesus wait before He began His journey to Bethany?

3. What evidence is there in this passage that Jesus knew Lazarus would be dead when He arrived?

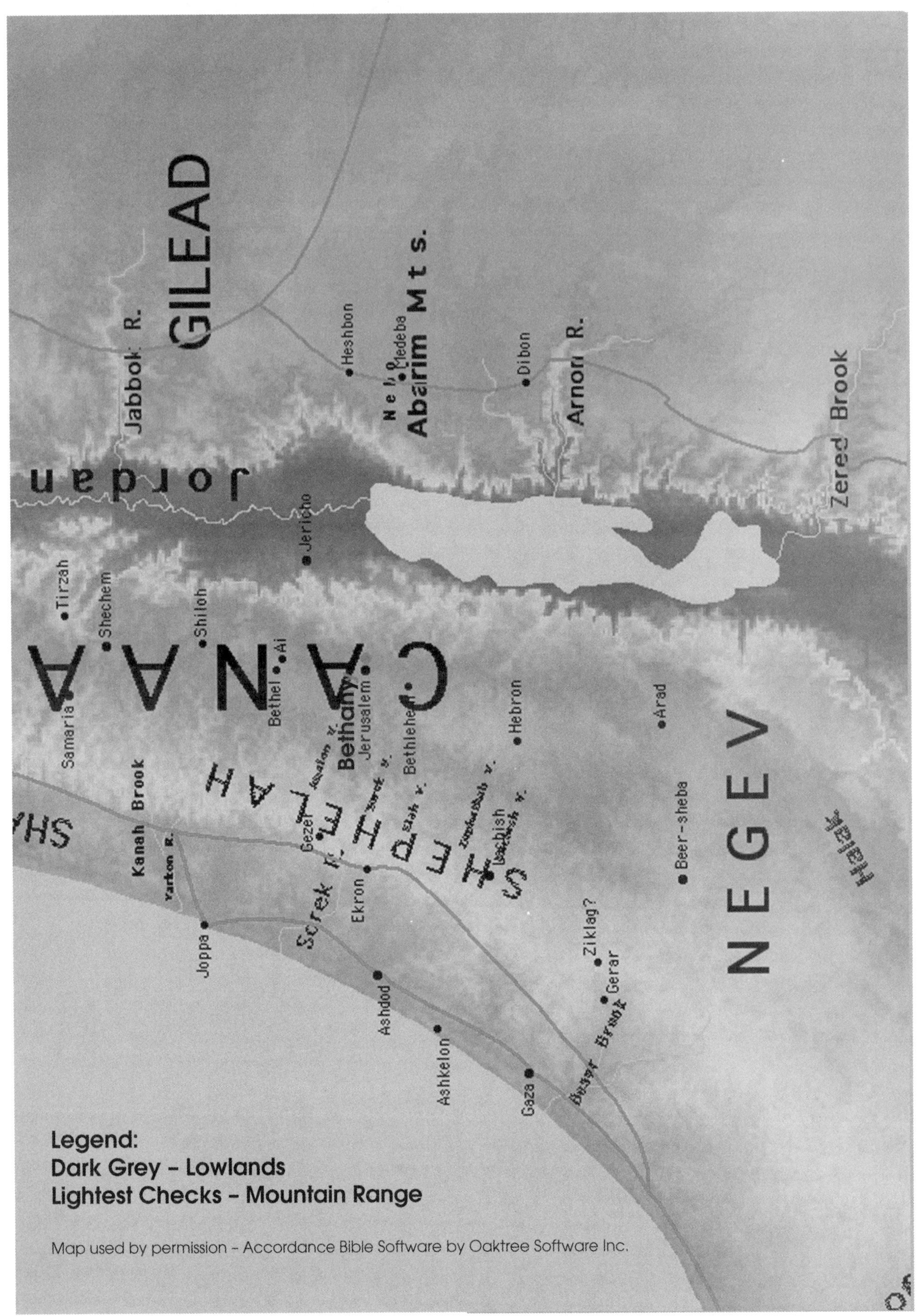

Map used by permission - Accordance Bible Software by Oaktree Software Inc.

Day 7

1. Read John 11:32-45. Answer the following questions in class. Write the answer to each question, then when everyone is finished, share your answers in class discussion.

(a) In verse 35 we read, "Jesus wept." Why do you think He was weeping?

(b) By this time Lazarus had been dead _________ days.

(c) Re-write Jesus' prayer in John 11:41-42 in your own words.

(d) Since we, like Mary and Martha, know Jesus could have healed Lazarus, why do you think He chose to delay until Lazarus was dead? Be specific. Give a scripture reference to support your answer.

2. Draw a sketch of Lazarus coming out of the tomb. Include the tomb in the background.

On Your Own: Answer the question and write the "Reflections."

John 11:45-53 gives two results of Jesus' demonstration of power. What were they?

Reflections: (1) Close your eyes and try to imagine how the Jews standing around the tomb felt when Jesus told them to unwrap the "grave clothes" that were on Lazarus. Write two to three sentences in your journal about your imagined feelings. Then write two to four sentences telling what you think you would have done in that situation.

(2) Think of an instance when God has shown His power on your behalf. Write about it in your journal.

(3) Remember you will have a quiz on Lesson 2 in two days. It will include your memory challenges.

Day 8

Guest Speaker

On Your Own: 1. Review your first memory challenge. Practice your second memory verse.

2. Have you ever thought that there might be some things God cannot do? Read the following passages and write what–according to the Bible–God cannot do.

(a) Hab. 1:13

(b) Titus 1:2

(c) 2 Tim. 2:13

(d) James 1:13

Day 9

1. Share your On Your Own answers in class.

2. Read Phil. 2:10. Because of God's great power, someday____________________________________ will bow before Him.

3. Close your eyes and picture this event. What demonstration of God's power might cause such a thing?

4. Which of these evidences of God's power do you consider greater–Elijah's burnt sacrifice or Lazarus' resurrection? Why?

5. You wrote in your journal two nights ago about a time when God showed His power on your behalf. If you are willing, share that experience with with your teacher.

On Your Own: You should be ready to write or recite all your memory challenges tomorrow. Also, tomorrow in class you will write a two-paragraph paper telling which demonstration of God's power recorded in the Bible you consider the greatest. The first paragraph should describe the incident, and the second should tell why you chose it. You may choose a story from the Old or New Testament. You may use your Bible to help you write the paper, but tonight you should make your choice and find the Bible reference. Please do not use either of the examples we studied in class. This is a graded assignment.

Day 10

1. Show your teacher the incident you chose and the Bible reference that records the incident.

2. Read the Writing Scoreboard.

3. Write your paper.

WRITING SCOREBOARD

1. Accuracy: Does the paragraph correctly tell the story? (30%)

2. Logic: Are good reasons given for the choice? (30%)

3. Organization. (15%)

4. Following directions. (15%)

5. Mechanics: Grammar, spelling, etc. (10%)

If you finish your paper early, you may read a library book.

On Your Own: Prepare for a test over Lesson 2 in two days.

Day 11

Review for your test by answering the questions on the study sheet.

On Your Own: Study for a test on Lesson 2.

Day 12

Test day.

Lesson 2–Study Sheet

1. Define: Awesome

   Omnipotent

   Taunt

2. How does God feel about wicked men, and why is He right to feel this way? Give a reference for your answers.

3. In this lesson we had reports on five natural disasters which demonstrated God's power. Name and briefly describe any four of them.

4. Write one sentence or phrase to identify each of the following.

(a) Obadiah

(b) Baal

(c) Bethany

(d) Lazarus

(e) Martha

5. Ahab was widely known for his ________________________ .

6. Ahab called Elijah the ___________________ of Israel.

7. What contest did Elijah propose between God and the false gods?

8. How many jars of water did they pour over Elijah's sacrifice?

9. List all the things God's fire burnt up completely.

10. At the end of this contest, what did the people do and say?

11. After the sisters asked Jesus to come to their home, how long did He wait before He began His journey?

12. What evidence is there in this passage that Jesus knew Lazarus would be dead when He arrived?

13. If He knew Lazarus would be dead, why was Jesus so slow in going to him?

14. What do you think Mary and Martha learned when Jesus raised their brother? Use scripture references to support your ideas.

15. Because of God's great power, someday ________ ________ ________ ________ before Jesus. In what book of the Bible is this statement found?

Reflections

Reflections

Reflections

Reflections

Reflections

Reflections

Reflections

The Hindu People

Image courtesy of PIONEERS

Varinasi, India, on the Ganges River, is the birthplace of the Hindu religion. Today most Hindus live in Asia (786,991,000). However, there are Hindus all over the world–even in the United States. The island of Bali, in Indonesia, is predominately Hindu, while the rest of Indonesia follows Muslim beliefs.

The Hindu People
Continued

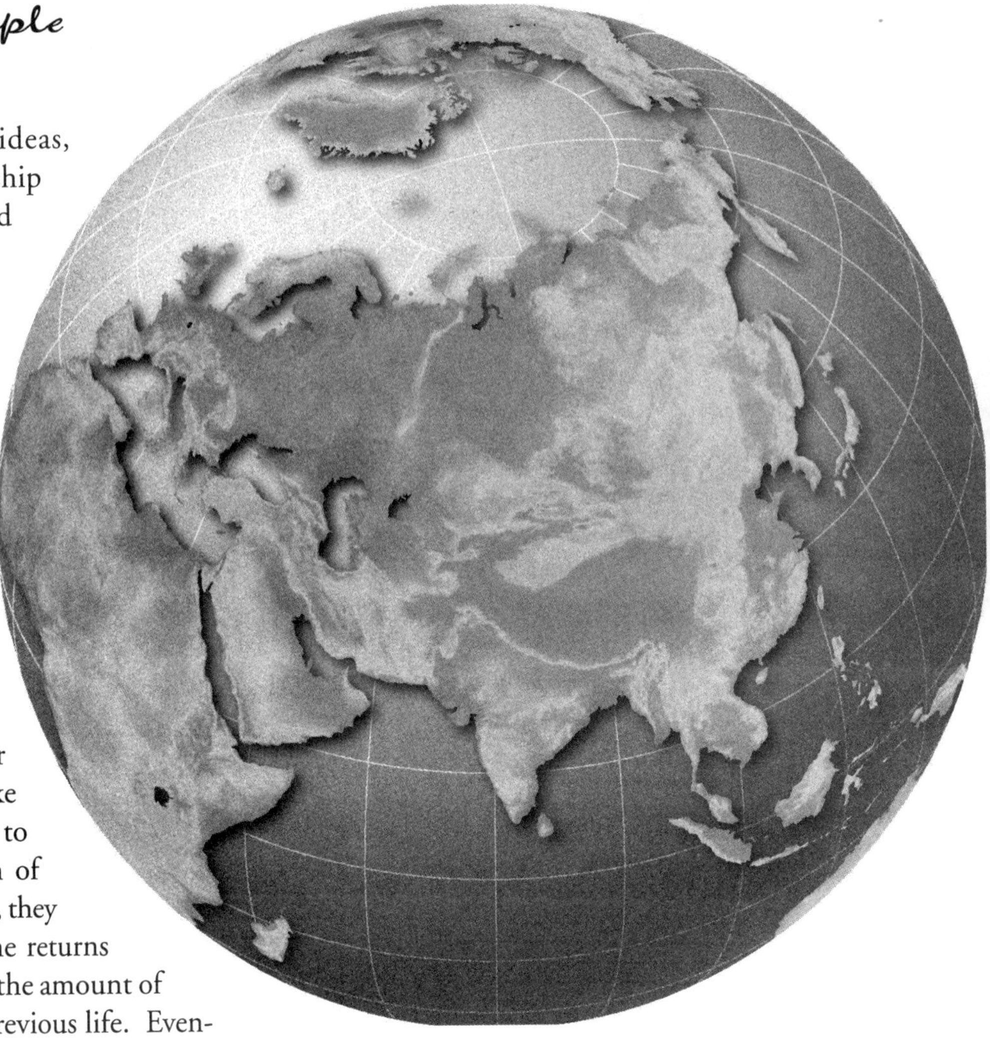

Hinduism is a mixture of many ideas, beliefs and practices. Hindus worship millions of gods, often dressing and giving food to their statues along every street and in the temples. Hindus believe that animals have souls and consider cows, monkeys, snakes, and other animals to be sacred. Cows even have the right of way, and cars must slowly go around them if they decide to lay down in the middle of a busy city street. Many of the images Hindus worship reflect these animals.

Hindus believe they can work their way to Heaven, although it may take several lifetimes or reincarnations to do it. Their religion is a religion of good works, and, like the Buddhists, they believe that when a person dies, he returns to life in some form depending on the amount of good deeds he performed in the previous life. Eventually, if a person is good enough, they believe that person will arrive in Heaven. Unfortunately for them, they are still unaware that the Bible says, *And as it is appointed unto men once to die, but after this the judgment.* Heb. 9:27

It is sad to realize that so many people are working very hard to earn something that they can never earn. Who will go and tell them that Jesus has already provided a way to Heaven for them?

Prayer Focus

That God would raise up missionaries to live in foreign countries to share the gospel with the Hindus.

That God would give people who have been saved out of the Hindu religion courage and patience to reach out to their friends and neighbors.

That God would draw Hindu people from all over the world to Himself.

Discovering God's Creativity

Memory Challenge

By faith we understand that the universe was formed at God's command, so that what is seen was not made out of what was visible. Heb. 11:3

When I was young, I thought all the colors in my 64-color crayon box were created by the crayon company. Then one day at a museum exhibit, I saw undersea coral for the first time. The starfish was bright, bright blue. The coral came in several shades of red. Tiny gold and green fish swam around. Suddenly, it dawned on me that God made colors. After that, the world never looked quite the same to me again. Wherever I looked, I saw something that God had created.

God's Word says:

You alone are the LORD. You made the heavens, even the highest heavens, and all their starry host, the earth and all that is on it, the seas and all that is in them. You give life to everything, and the multitudes of heaven worship you. Neh. 9:6

1. Write down the name of the most creative person you know. Under the name, list three things that person has created. Note: This could be something created in art, music, drama, writing, carpentry, needlework, mechanics, computer, etc.

2. Would you have room on one piece of paper to list all the things that person has created?

How many pieces of paper would you need?

3. How many pieces of paper would you need to list all the things God has created?

4. God is the supreme creator. We could make up a word for that–omni-creative. He is the first and greatest creator. He is also the source of all creativity. Think about the person whose name you wrote on your paper. Where did that person get his/her creativity?

Read Gen. 1:26-27. What or who is the source of all creativity?

The ability we have to create is one way we are like God. I used to say, "I can't do that. I'm not creative." Then one day I thought, "Well, who is the source of creativity?" God showed me that creativity is a gift from Him. Since that time, whenever I need a creative idea, I ask God to give me one!

On Your Own: Study the memory challenge.

Day 2

1. Yesterday, we said one way we are made in God's image is that we are also ______________________

____.

2. Of course, there is a difference in our creative ability and God's. To test this, let's imagine we're going to create something. What would you like to create?

3. Now that we've agreed on what we're going to create, let's make a list of all the things we need to create this object.

4. What is the problem that makes our creative task different than God's?

On Your Own: Read Gen. 1:26-2:2. Answer the following questions.

1. What did God use to create the earth and the heavens?

2. How did God create each thing? (Give a reference.)

3. What did God NOT make?

4. How did God feel about what He had made? Read Ps. 135:6 to find out.

Day 3

1. Read Gen. 1:26-2:2. Go over your On Your Own questions with your teacher.

Do you enjoy science class? When I was your age, I hated science. But one day God showed me that science is just the study of the things He created. When you think of science in that way, it's fascinating.

2. Write down something you consider to be one of God's most fascinating creations, then write three reasons for your choice. Discuss your choices with the class.

3. When God talks to Job near the end of the book of Job, He gives a detailed description of some of His creations. Read Job 41:1, 8-9, 12-34.

Use the details in this description to draw a picture of the leviathan. There are at least six details you should include. Hint: This is a four-legged animal. When everyone is finished, compare your pictures.

Scholars disagree about what animal is being described here. Some say it is the crocodile. Others think it is some type of dinosaur, possibly even a model of the mythical dragon.

4. It is interesting to try to picture this animal, but God put this description in His Word to make a point. To learn the point He is making, read verses 10-11. What does God want us to learn from this description of the leviathan?

On Your Own: Read Ps. 104:5-9 and rewrite it in your own words. If it contains words you don't know, look them up. Hint: you might want to read these verses in two or three translations before you rewrite them.

Day 4

1. Read your rewriting of the verses from Psalms to your teacher.

2. Watch a video.

Reflections: Write at least ten sentences in your journal sharing your thoughts about the video and about God's creativity.

You will be graded on your memory challenge tomorrow.

Day 5

1. God's creation tells us a great deal about Him. What are some truths about God's character you think we might learn from creation?

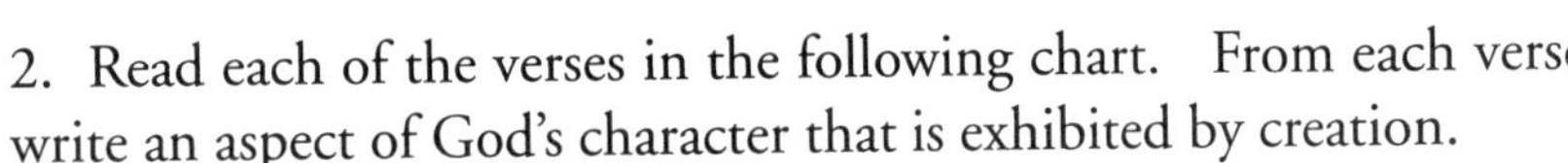
2. Read each of the verses in the following chart. From each verse write an aspect of God's character that is exhibited by creation.

Reference	Characteristic Exhibited
(a) Ps. 33:5	
(b) Ps. 104:24, 136:5	
(c) Ps. 145:10, 148:5	
(d) Isa. 40:26-28	
(e) Rom. 1:20	

On Your Own: Review the following scriptures and answer the questions.

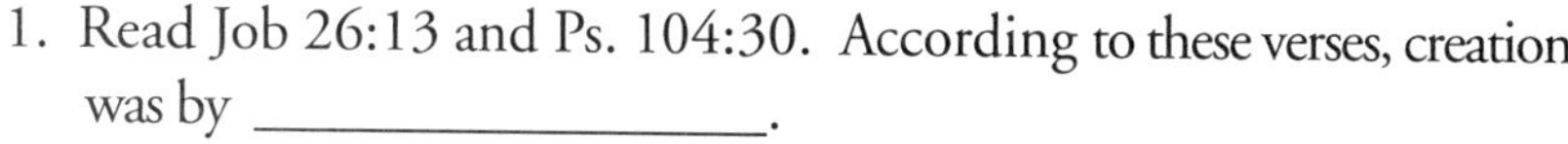

1. Read Job 26:13 and Ps. 104:30. According to these verses, creation was by ________________.

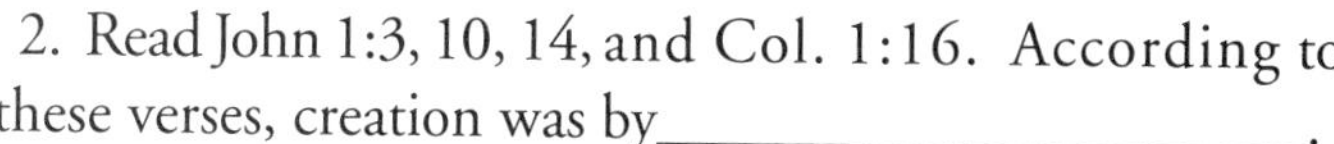

2. Read John 1:3, 10, 14, and Col. 1:16. According to these verses, creation was by____________________.

3. Read Gen. 1:26. According to this verse, who created man?

4. Explain these different answers.

Day 6

I praise you because I am fearfully and wonderfully made;
your works are wonderful, I know that full well. Ps. 139:14

Your science and Bible classes will share a project to increase your understanding of God's marvelous creativity. Begin that project today. It will be due when you come to class three days from now.

On Your Own: Work on your project.

Day 7

1. Practice your memory challenge.
2. Work on your science/Bible project.

On Your Own: Work on your project.

Day 8

1. Practice Ps. 139:14. You will be graded on all your memory challenges three days from now.

2. Work on your science/Bible project. This project will be due tomorrow.

On Your Own: Finish your project.

Day 9

Turn in your science/Bible project. Present your project in class.

On Your Own: Take a nature walk. Make a list of all the different colors you see. You may need to name some of the colors. For example: geranium red or new-grass green. Or you can just describe them, for example: bright, bright red or almost-purple blue. (This will help you appreciate the problems the Crayola manufacturers have coming up with exact names for crayons.) Collect at least 25 colors. Be sure all the colors come from nature, not from the paint on your house or the toys in your driveway.

Day 10

God not only made this earth we enjoy, He will make a new heaven and a new earth. Read Rev. 21:10-23.

C. S. Lewis had a theory that in the new earth all the colors will be brighter and more beautiful than they are on this earth, but we'll have to use what we have. Using the verses in Revelation, draw the New Jerusalem. Color the city, including the gemstones that are inlaid in each layer of the wall. You may work in pairs to look up the colors you aren't familiar with. As you do this, remember the New Jerusalem is just one more example of God's endless creativity.

On Your Own: Study your memory challenges. You will be tested on *all* of them at the end of this lesson.

Day 11

1. One of the most creative things God made is man. Read Ps. 139:13-18.

(a) According to David, who made him?

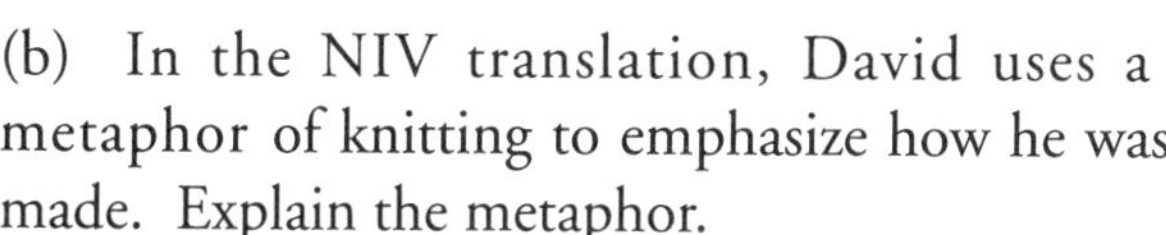

(b) In the NIV translation, David uses a metaphor of knitting to emphasize how he was made. Explain the metaphor.

(c) Which verse tells you when God first knew David? Explain that verse.

2. Have you ever thought about the wonderful creativity God displayed in the creation of man? Think about the wonder of your own body. Hold out your hand and wiggle your fingers. Notice how the tendons and muscles cooperate with each other to control your finger movements. Look in a mirror and admire your face. Notice how God gave you ears on both sides of your head so you can hear sounds from all directions. Close one eye and notice how you lose depth perception. Aren't you glad God gave you two eyes? As you study the human body in science, you will learn more and more about how "fearfully and wonderfully" we are made.

(a) Why did God give you such a wonderfully made body?

(b) What does He expect you to do with it?

(c) How do you think God feels when His children abuse the bodies He has made?

3. Write a psalm that praises God for His creativity.

On Your Own: Study all your memory challenges. Be prepared to write or recite them for a grade on the day after tomorrow.

Day 12

Take a field trip. While you are on the trip, think about God's endless creativity. Think about how God's creativity is related to His power. We will talk about that tomorrow.

Reflections: Either on the way back to school, or at home tonight, write in your journal what you observed about God's creativity. Tomorrow we will discuss your observations in class. You will also be graded on all your memory challenges tomorrow.

Day 13

1. Recite or write all your memory challenges for a grade.

2. Share your journal entry on what you observed about God's creativity and power on the field trip.

3. Talk about the relationship between God's creativity and His power.

4. Answer the questions on the study sheet to help you prepare for the test tomorrow.

On Your Own: Study for the test tomorrow.

Day 14

Take a test.

Lesson 3–Study Sheet

1. The source of all creativity is ________.
2. One way that we are made in God's image is ____.
3. Describe a leviathan.
4. What does God want us to learn from the biblical description of the leviathan?
5. List and briefly describe at least five aspects of God's character that we can see in creation.
6. David compared the way God made him to the way someone might ______________________.
7. According to Ps. 139, when did God first know David?

8. Essay–write a short paragraph to answer each of the following questions.

(a) Why did God give you such a wonderful body?

(b) Explain how God's creativity and power are related.

(c) Describe the New Jerusalem. Tell where in the Bible you find this description.

Reflections

Reflections

Reflections

Reflections

The Chinese People

Image courtesy of PIONEERS

Did you know China has over one billion citizens? In addition to the Han Chinese who share a written language and make up the majority of the population, there are at least 55 minority groups in China. They each have distinctive dress, language, and culture, and in some ways they are considered tribal. These minority groups are looked down on by government officials who often discriminate against them.

The Chinese People
Continued

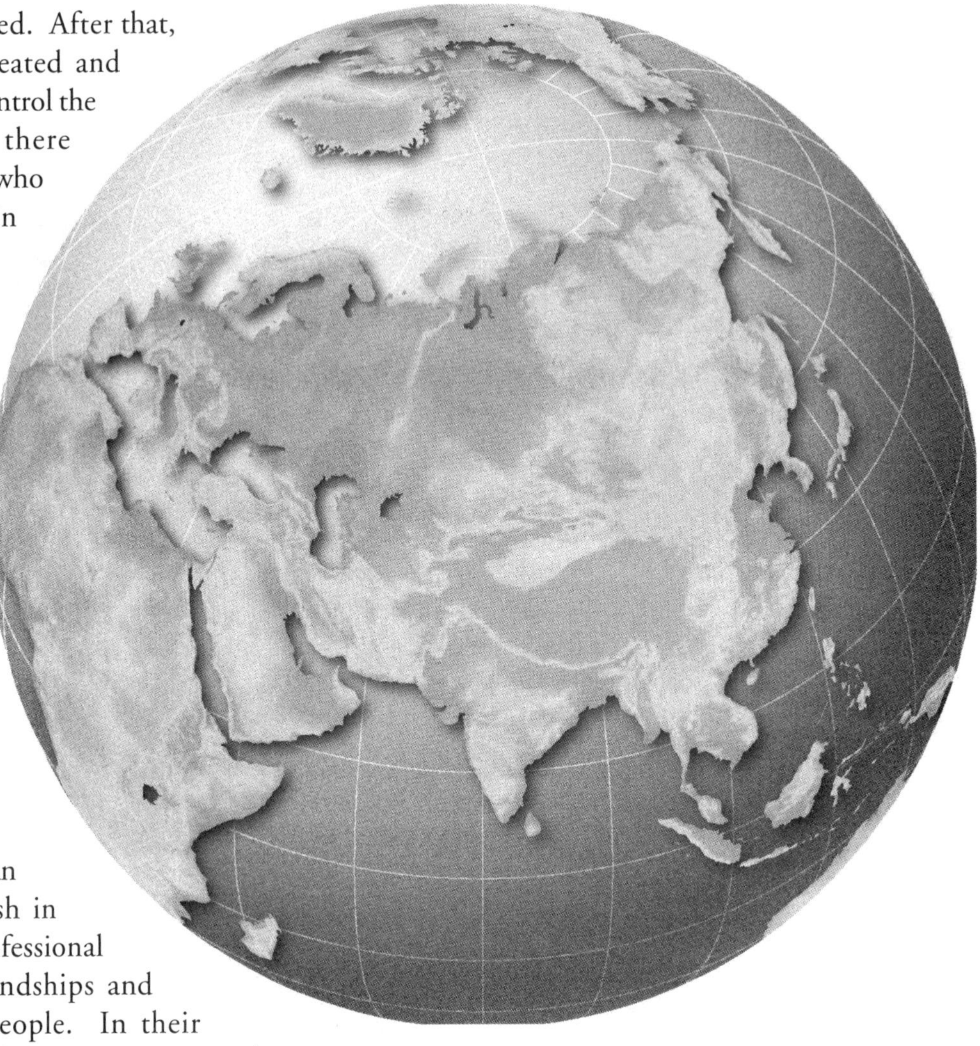

Communism swept through China after World War II, and missionaries were expelled. After that, Chinese Christians were mistreated and sometimes killed by those who control the government. In spite of this, there are millions of people in China who quietly and discretely believe in Christ. Yet Chinese Christians make up only a small percentage of the vast population of China. Many Chinese have substituted Communism for their religion. Others are animists (believing that different gods live in things in nature), followers of strange cults, ancestor worshipers, or atheists. In all these beliefs, the Chinese people are searching for God– they are just searching in the wrong places.

Christians from other countries can work in China teaching English in universities or in a variety of professional jobs in order to establish friendships and build bridges with Chinese people. In their changing world today, many of them are open to the gospel. We Christians need to be bold and unselfish to take advantage of this openness and carry the gospel to China while we can.

Prayer Focus

That the "door" to China would remain open to "creative access" workers.

That Christians would be willing to live in China to reach the Han and the ethnic minority peoples with the gospel.

That God would make the Chinese Christians "wise as serpents and harmless as doves" as they witness to their neighbors.

Discovering God's Love

Memory	*I have loved you with an everlasting love; I have drawn you with loving-kindness.* Jer. 31: 3b *How great is the love the Father has lavished on us, that we should be called children of God! And that is what we are!* 1 John 3:1a	Challenge

We talk of love often–I love chocolate; I love pizza; I love my dog. We say "I love you" to a boyfriend or girlfriend very easily, some of us to a different one every month.

But God is serious about love. When He says, "I have loved you with an everlasting love..." in Jer. 31:3, He means it. The apostle John wrote, "God is love." 1 John 4:16. God's character is the very definition of love.

Hopefully you will spend the rest of your life learning more and more about God's love. For now, let's see how much we can learn in the next three weeks.

1. Write your definition of love.

2. Write a dictionary definition of love. You will find many ideas for love in the dictionary. Write five of them.

3. Read the two memory challenges for this week.

(a) What does *everlasting* mean?

(b) Look up the context of the memory verse in Jeremiah. Who is talking in this verse, and who is His message for?

(c) Define *lavish*.

(d) Who are the "children of God"? Read Rom. 8:14-16 to help you with the answer.

(e) What do you think is the best definition for love as it is used in these two verses?

4. Write two important things you have learned about God's love from these two verses.

Stop and thank God for these great truths!

On Your Own: To see a biblical definition of love, read 1 Cor. 13:4-7 and answer the following questions.

In these verses, God tells us what love is, what it does not do, and finally what it always does.

1. Verse 4 lists two things that love is. List each one and define it in your own words.

2. Next, Paul lists eight things that love does NOT do. List each one and then restate it with positive words. For an example, see the chart below.

What Love Does Not...	What Love Does...
Love does not envy.	Love is glad when someone else has something good.

3. In your own words, list the four things that love always does.

4. Choose someone in your life–family or friends–that you can perform an action of love for this week. Write their name in your journal. Make it your goal to do one action of love each day. Four days from now, you will report on what you did and the results.

Day 2

1. Think about the things you read about love in 1 Cor. 13. What do these verses say about the *feelings* of love?

2. Read the poem on the following page and answer the questions below.

(a) What is the point of the poem?

(b) Explain how this is also the point of 1 Cor. 13.

3. In the box below write the third important thing you have learned about love.

Thank God for this truth about His love.

Suzie's Several Suitors

Suitor #1

"I love you, Suzie."
He kissed her cheek.
"You sure are a lot of fun."

"Thanks for the cookin',
The trouble you took." and
Then with a look

At the pots and pans in the kitchen sink...

"So sorry, I gotta' run.

Can't help you clean,
Well–you know–I mean...
Gotta' meet with the team.

The warm-up's already begun."

Suitor #2

"I love you, Suzie."
He gave her a squeeze.
"You're the best little cook I know."

"That meal was a treat
Didn't know I could eat
So much. You're so sweet...

"Oh, those pots and pans in the kitchen sink...

So sorry I gotta' go.

I'd sure do my part, but
Deer season just started.
I'll be broken-hearted

If I don't get a shot at a doe."

Suitor #3

"I love you, Suzie."
He gazed at her face.
"You've made this a lovely time.

"You're so kind to invite me;
Your sauces delight me.
The roast beef was just right...

"But those pots and pans in the kitchen sink,

Now that's a job I can share!

You've given your time,
Now I'll give of mine.
It's not hard I find;

The pleasure's in showing I care."

* * * * * * *

Our Suzie, at last, has a suitor who knows
Love's not just what you say, it's more what you show!

Usually when I read 1 Cor. 13, I am thinking of it as things I should do for others. I should be more patient; I should be more kind; etc. That is a valid way to look at this passage, but today, let's look at these verses in I Cor. 13 in a different way. Let's think of these as characteristics that God shows toward us.

On Your Own: 1. Reread the characteristics of love from vv. 4-7 listed in the chart below. For each characteristic, spend some time thinking about God, and how He demonstrates or has demonstrated that characteristic toward you. Then choose **five** of these characteristics and write an example of how God has demonstrated each one of the five in your own life.

Characteristic of God's Love	Demonstrated to me when God...
Patient	
Kind	
Not selfish	
Not easily angered	
Keeps no record of wrongs	
Rejoices in the truth	
Protective	
Hopeful	
Persevering	

2. In the box write your two favorite truths about God's love that you learned from 1 Cor. 13.

Thank God for these favorite truths.

Day 3

The Bible says all the things that happened in the Old Testament are to be lessons and examples for us. For an enlightening picture of God's love, let's study the Old Testament story of Jacob and Rachel.

1. Read Gen. 29:15-30.

(a) What was the relationship between Jacob and Laban?

(b) Which of Laban's daughters was Jacob attracted to first? Why?

(c) What agreement did Jacob make with Laban?

(d) At the end of the seven years, Laban prepared a surprise for Jacob. What was the surprise?

(e) Jacob, you may remember, was a deceitful man who had tricked both his brother and his father. How is his relationship with Laban ironic?

(f) Jacob was not willing to give up Rachel. In their culture, multiple wives were acceptable–even common, so what new contract did Jacob make with Laban?

(g) How many years did Jacob work altogether to earn the wife that he loved?

2. Remembering that these things happened as a lesson to us, write at least two sentences explaining how Jacob's love for Rachel is a picture of God's love for us. (If you need to refresh your memory on the characteristics of love, you may refer to the chart on page 82.)

3. In the box, write the important truth you learned about God's love from the story of Jacob and Rachel.

Thank God for this special truth.

Reflections: In your journal, write a paragraph or two about how God has persevered in loving you. Study your memory challenge verses. They will be due the day after tomorrow.

Day 4

From the Psalms of the Bible to the praise choruses we sing today, many Christians express their appreciation for God's love with music. Today we will read and discuss two hymns that were written about God's love.

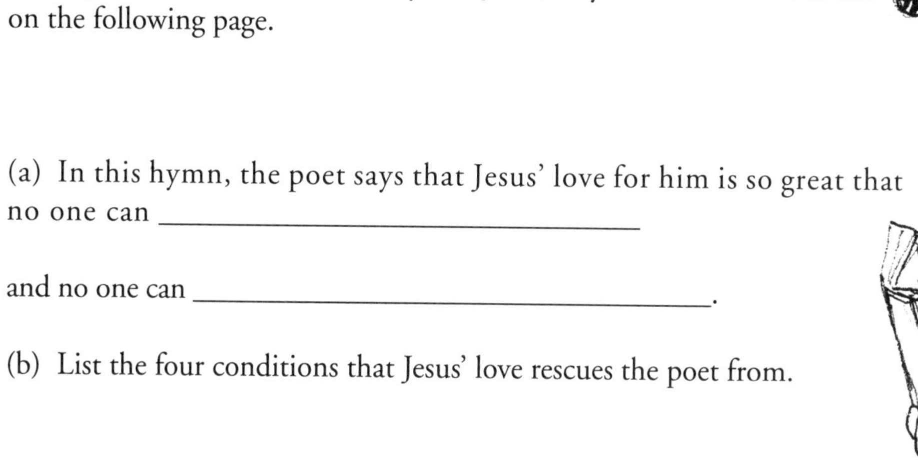

1. Sing or read the words to the hymn "Jesus, Thy Boundless Love to Me" on the following page.

(a) In this hymn, the poet says that Jesus' love for him is so great that no one can ______________________________

and no one can ______________________________.

(b) List the four conditions that Jesus' love rescues the poet from.

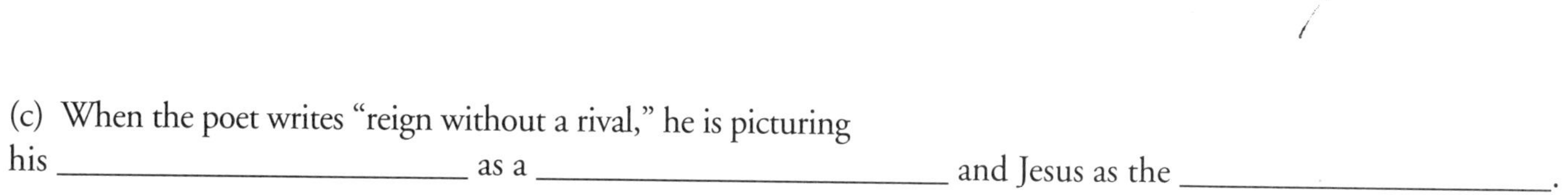

(c) When the poet writes "reign without a rival," he is picturing his ______________________ as a ______________________ and Jesus as the ______________________.

(d) In this picture, what could be a *rival* to Jesus?

2. Sing or read "Love Divine, All Loves Excelling" on the next page.

(a) What does "excelling" mean as it is used in this context?

Jesus, Thy Boundless Love to Me

Ephesians 3:18

By: Paul Gerhardt

Jesus, thy boundless love to me
No tho't can reach, no tongue declare;
O knit my thankful heart to thee,
And reign without a rival there:
Thine wholly, thine alone, I am;
Be thou alone my constant flame.

O Love, how gracious is thy way!
All fear before thy presence flies;
Care, anguish, sorrow melt away,
Where'er thy healing beams arise:
O Jesus, nothing may I see,
Nothing desire, or seek, but thee.

Love Divine, All Loves Excelling

1John 4:16
By: Charles Wesley, 1747

Love divine, all loves excelling,
Joy of heaven, to earth come down!
Fix in us Thy humble dwelling,
All Thy faithful mercies crown.
Jesus, Thou art all compassion,
Pure, unbounded love Thou art;
Visit us with Thy salvation,
Enter ev'ry trembling heart.

Breathe, O breathe Thy loving spirit
Into ev'ry troubled breast;
Let us all in Thee inherit,
Let us find Thy promised rest.
Take away the love of sinning;
Alpha and Omega be;
End of faith, as its beginning,
Set our hearts at liberty.

(b) Who is the poet addressing (talking to) in this poem?

(c) How do you know?

(d) In the first stanza, the writer addresses Jesus by two "titles" which describe Jesus' character. The first one is "Love divine." What is the second one? Explain what the second one means.

(e) In the first stanza, the writer describes Christ as "pure, unbounded love." What does he mean by that phrase?

(f) In the second stanza, what does the author ask Christ to "take away."?

(g) What do Alpha and Omega mean? (Hint: Use the context of the next line to help figure it out.)

(h) How is Jesus the Alpha and the Omega?

On Your Own: Write a poem using comparisons or word pictures to describe God's love. Your poem should be at least twelve lines long.

2. Be prepared to write or recite your memory challenge for a grade tomorrow.

Day 5

1. Share your poem.

2. Read Psalm 89:1-2, 14-16.

(a) What three verbs does the writer use to tell what he is going to do?

(b) Some of the words that the poet uses to describe God in vv. 1-2 are repeated in v. 14. What are those words?

(c) According to this Psalm, how long will God's love last?

3. Write a psalm of your own about God's love. Try to follow the pattern of Psalm 89.

Reflections: Write a paragraph or two about the person you chose to show love toward this week. Explain what you did and what happened.

Day 6

Memory Challenge

Greater love has no one than this, that one lay down his life for his friends. John 15:13

But God demonstrates his own love for us in this:
While we were still sinners, Christ died for us. Rom. 5:8

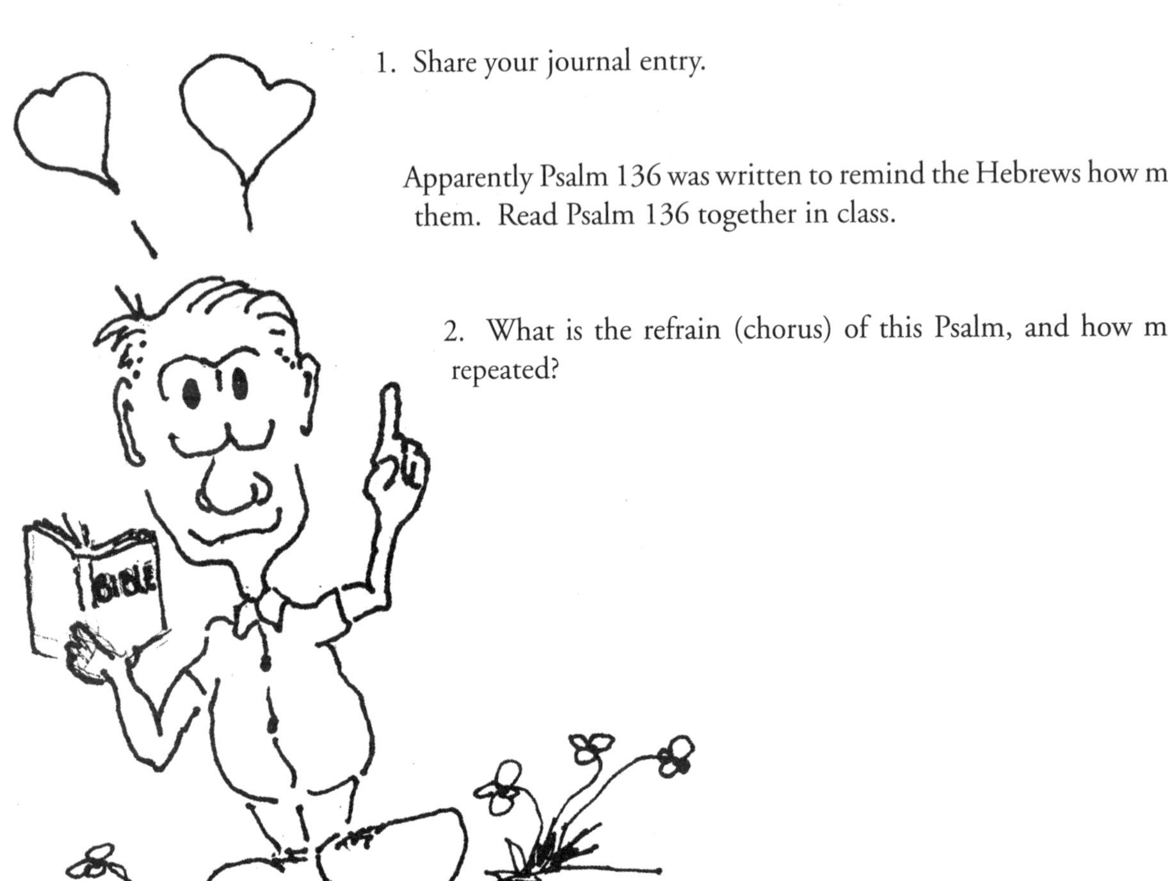

1. Share your journal entry.

Apparently Psalm 136 was written to remind the Hebrews how much God loved them. Read Psalm 136 together in class.

2. What is the refrain (chorus) of this Psalm, and how many times is it repeated?

3. This Psalm has an introduction (vv. 1-3) and a conclusion (vv. 23-26). The remaining part can be divided into three sections. Write the subject of each section in the following chart.

(a) vv. 4-9	
(b) vv. 10-15	
(c) vv. 16-22	

4. According to Psalm 136, how long will God love us?

5. According to this Psalm, what should our response be to God's love? Give a reference.

6. Explain why this response is a logical one.

7. One of the points Psalm 136 makes is that we know how much God loves us based on

____

____ .

This relates to the verses we read in 1 Cor. 13 because those verses pointed out that love is not how we ____________________ but rather what

we ________________________________ .

Reflections: God also says He can tell how much we love Him (or don't love Him) based on something we do (or don't do.) Read John 14:15. Write a paragraph in your journal explaining how you can demonstrate your love for Jesus.

Day 7

1. Share your journal entry if you choose.

2. Look up the context of John 15:13 to answer the following questions.

(a) Who is talking?

(b) Who is He talking to?

(c) What is the setting? (See also John 13:1-2.)

(d) What could Jesus be referring to in these verses?

3. Read Rom. 5:6-8.

(a) Paul is saying here that someone might be willing to die for another person who is ____________________.

(b) Can you think of an example of someone who might die to save another person?

Jesus says a man who deeply loves a friend might die for that friend. Compare the verse from John with the verse from Romans in the question below.

4. Jesus' love goes beyond dying for ________________ because He also died for ________________ .

5. Romans 5:8 and John 3:16 state the heart of the gospel message. Read these verses and write down how you would explain the gospel message to an unbeliever who sincerely wanted to know how to be saved.

On Your Own: 1. Write a paragraph or two clearly explaining three specific differences in your life based on the fact that Jesus loved you enough to die on the cross for you.

2. In three days you will be tested on **all** the memory challenge verses you have had this semester. You should begin reviewing them now.

Day 8

1. Share your paragraph.

2. The Israelites had a special ceremony every year to remind them of God's love in delivering them from Egypt.

(a) What did they call this feast?

(b) Read Ex. 12:1-13 to review the first Passover meal.

3. Right before Jesus was arrested, He was celebrating the Passover feast with his disciples. Read John 13:1-5; Matt. 26:20-21, 26-30; Luke 22:7-8, 14-20. Make a list of the things Jesus and the disciples did to celebrate the Passover.

On Your Own: Using the following verses, research the Passover (Feast of Unleavened Bread) and fill in the first three lines of the following chart. We will finish the chart in class tomorrow.

In addition, try to find out *when* the Jews celebrated this feast, and *why* they celebrated it. We will compare notes in class tomorrow and then plan our own Passover meal. Verses: Ex. 12:1-13, Lev. 23:4-8, Deu. 16:2, 5-7.

The Passover was celebrated in the ________(time of year).

The food they ate	What that food symbolized

Don't forget to review your memory challenges!

Day 9

1. Compare notes on the Passover. Do more research in library books, and add more foods to your chart.

2. As you read the research books, also watch for any special actions the Israelites took during the Passover meal and explain these actions.

Special actions	What the actions symbolized

3. Plan a Passover meal.

(a) Make a list of people to invite.

(b) Make a list of food to serve.

(c) Make a list of who is responsible for what.

On Your Own:

1. Put together your Bible costume for the Passover meal.

2. Study all your memory challenge verses. Be ready to write or recite them tomorrow.

Day 10

Write or recite all your memory challenge verses.

Make preparations for the Passover meal.

On Your Own: Remember to wear your Bible costume tomorrow.

Day 11

Celebrate the Passover.

Reflections: What was the most meaningful part of the Passover ceremony for you? Write a paragraph or two.

Day 12

1. To help you summarize the lessons about God's love, write the answers to the following thought questions on your own. When everyone is finished, we will discuss the answers in class.

(a) Why did the Israelites celebrate the Passover?

(b) What special celebration do Christians have today that is related to the Passover?

(c) Explain how the two celebrations are related.

(d) Explain how our Christian celebration is related to God's love.

2. God is all-powerful, all-wise, and totally creative. We are very unpowerful, often unwise, and have limited creativity, yet God loves us.

(a) WHY does God love you?

(b) Think of all these characteristics of God together and explain what it means to you that the God who loves you is also powerful, wise, and creative.

Reflections

Reflections

Reflections

The Secular People

Image courtesy of PIONEERS

There has always been a group of people who claim to have no religion. They believe that man is in charge of his own destiny and that there is no Heaven or Hell. Often we call these people atheists.

The Secular People
Continued

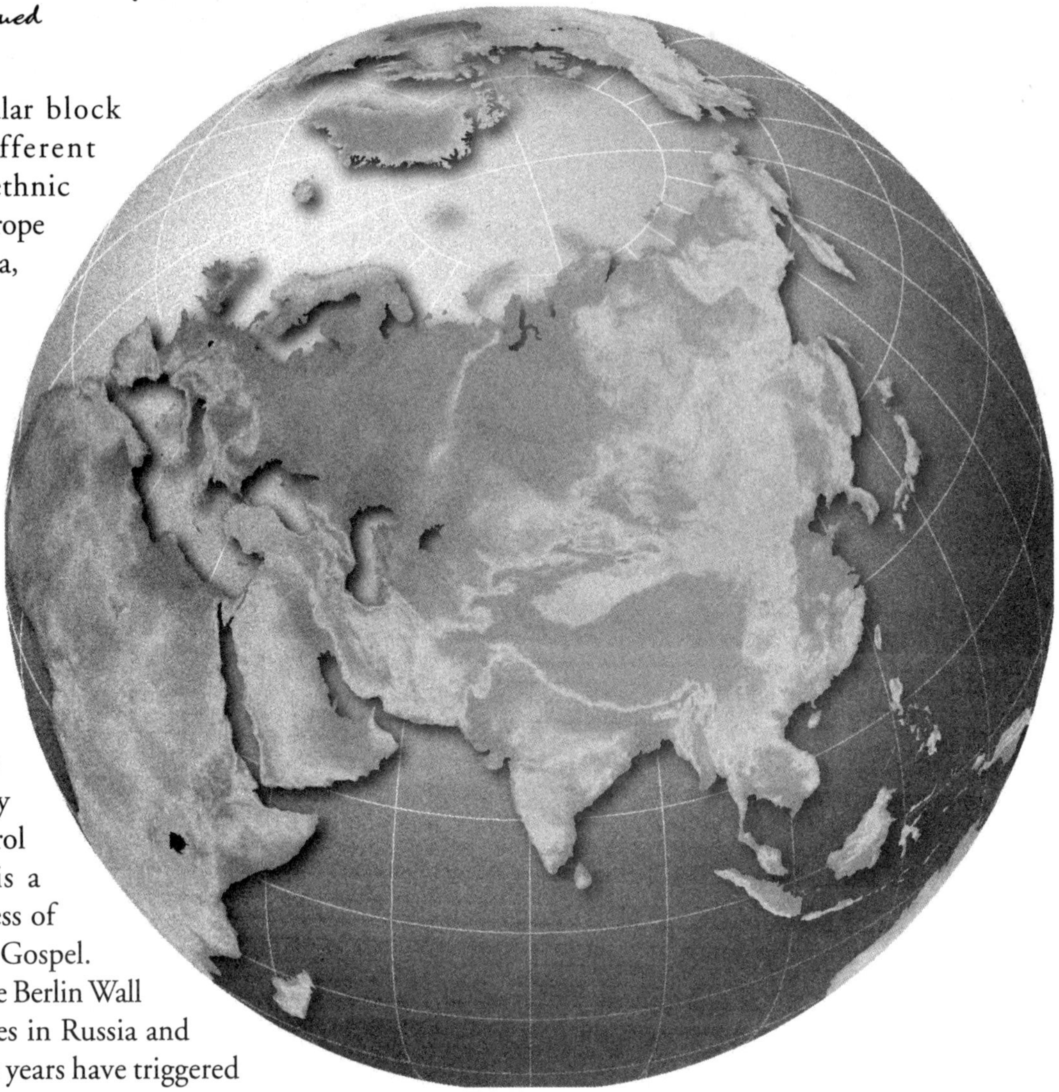

The people in the secular block come from many different races, countries, and ethnic groups. From Eastern Europe to North Korea to Russia, secular people can be found everywhere. Through the effects of humanistic influence in our education and school system, we have many secular people who do not believe in God in our own country.

As recent historical events have shown people all over the world that they actually have little control over their lives, there is a new and special openness of the secular block to the Gospel. For example, the fall of the Berlin Wall and the sweeping changes in Russia and other countries in recent years have triggered a deep sense of the failure of atheistic Communism in many countries.

Secular people will only find security and peace in Jesus. How can we help them discover the truth they need?

Prayer Focus

That Christians will move quickly to take advantage of current political trends and reach out to the hungry hearts in former Communist countries.

That God will maintain the openness to His Word that exists today.

That Christians will make the most of the present openness of secular people everywhere.

Discovering God's Holiness

Memory Challenge

Oh LORD our God, you answered them; you were to Israel a forgiving God, though you punished their misdeeds. Exalt the LORD our God and worship at his holy mountain, for the LORD our God is holy. **Ps. 99:8-9**

God is holy. God's holiness sets Him apart and lifts Him up above all creation. The Bible asks, *Who among the gods is like you, O LORD? Who is like you–majestic in holiness, awesome in glory, working wonders?* (Ex. 15:11)

The word *holiness* tells us that God is perfectly moral and perfectly ethical. He is *separated* from everything evil and sinful.

God's love is holy love; His power is holy power; His wisdom is holy wisdom.

What do you think *holy* means?

1. Write your own definition of holy.

2. Write the dictionary definition of holy.

3. According to Bible dictionaries, holy means separate, different, bright, pure, righteous, morally perfect.

Which of these definitions best agrees with your idea of God's holiness? Explain your reasons in one or two complete sentences.

4. Which Bible dictionary ideas are different than the ones in the regular dictionary?

5. Re-read the dictionary definition and try to add these ideas of holiness to the ones you already have. Revise your original definition.

6. Read Isaiah 6:1-7. This is a very dramatic scene. Try to picture each detail in your imagination.

(a) How do you think Isaiah saw the Lord? (That is, a dream, a vision, he was lifted up to heaven, etc.)

(b) Where was the Lord? In a ____________________, on a ________________________. (v. 1)

(c) What kind of angels were there?

On Your Own: Using a concordance, look up as many verses as you can find that mention cherubim and/or seraphs. Fill in the following chart. Note the reference after each entry you make.

What they look like.	What they do.	Where they are seen.
Seraphs (KJV, Seraphims)		
Cherubim		

Day 2

1. Share the results of your On Your Own assignment in class.

2. Re-read Isaiah 6:1-7. Do you remember the scene as we discussed it yesterday? Briefly review, then continue with the following questions.

(a) Why did the seraphs cover their eyes?

(b) What were they saying to one another?

(c) How did Isaiah feel in v. 5?

(d) Why did he feel this way?

(e) One of the seraphs put a hot coal on Isaiah's lips. What do you think the coal symbolized? (Hint: Think about where the coal came from.)

(f) What is the point of this passage?

(g) Read Job 42:1-6 and Luke 5:1-8. Write a short paragraph telling a valuable truth we can learn from these two passages and the verses we have studied from Isaiah.

On Your Own: The Bible talks about seraphs and cherubim as two types of angels. Use the information in Isaiah 6:1-7 plus information from your chart and from a Bible dictionary to draw a sketch of a seraph. Or, if you prefer, use the references and information in your chart to sketch a cherub.

Day 3

1. Share your pictures and discuss the details of the angels' appearance.

2. Review. What things in the passage from Isaiah emphasize God's holiness?

3. Remember that a psalm is actually a ______________________________.

4. Look up "exalted" and write out the definition.

5. Read Ps. 99 and answer the following questions.

(a) What is the "chorus" of this Psalm?

(b) Right before each chorus is a command. Write the three commands and give the reference for each.

(c) In each command, we are told to praise and worship God because He is ______________________________ .

(d) How is the picture in v. 1 similar to the picture in Isaiah 6?

(e) Each section of this song has a statement about God. Read the verse indicated and write that statement.

Section 1, v. 2–

Section 2, v. 4–

Section 3, v. 8–

(f) All of these characteristics of God are brought together by the characteristic that is repeated in the chorus–God is ______________________________________ .

Reflections: Spend ten minutes thinking about God's holiness. Then write your thoughts in your journal.

Day 4

1. Read Exodus 19:10-15.

(a) What is the setting of this passage?

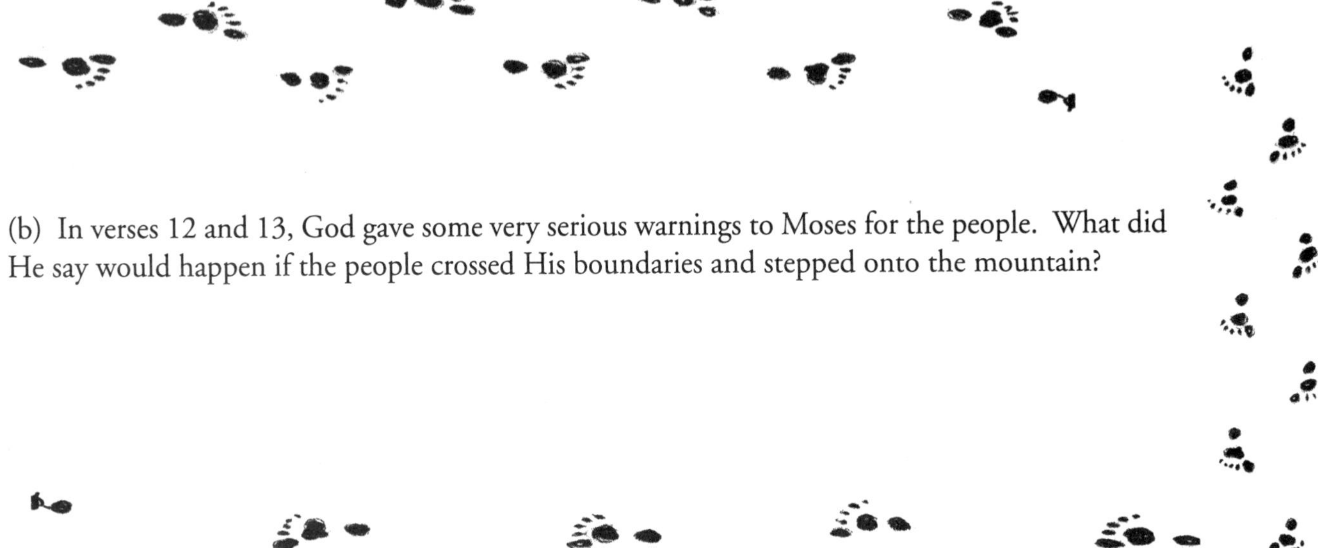

(b) In verses 12 and 13, God gave some very serious warnings to Moses for the people. What did He say would happen if the people crossed His boundaries and stepped onto the mountain?

(c) Why do you think God put such strong restrictions on the people? (See Isa. 59:2 and Hab. 1:13a.)

2. Read Ex. 19:16-25.

(a) Describe the scene in v. 16.

(b) How did the people feel about what they were seeing and hearing?

How do you know?

(c) We know that we cannot see God, but what tangible signs of His presence are found in verses 18 and 19?

(d) God was very insistent that Moses warn the people a second time. Why do you think God repeated His warning and insisted that Moses talk to the people again?

3. What similarities can you find in these verses in Exodus and the passages in Isaiah and Psalms that we studied previously?

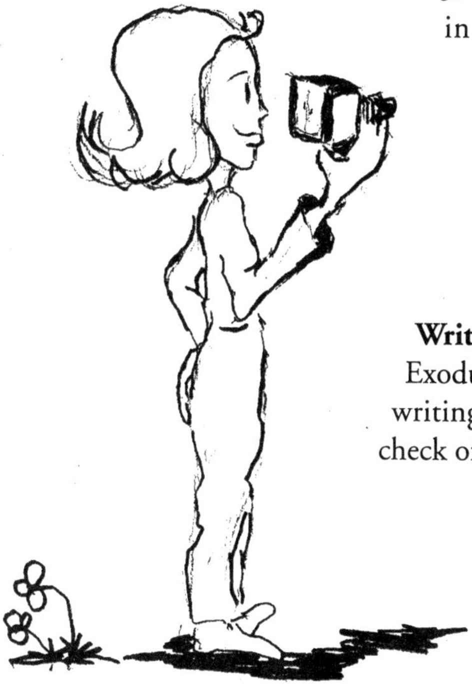

Writing Opportunity: Choose either the scene from Isaiah or the scene from Exodus to write as a screen play (a script for a movie.) We will do the actual writing in class tomorrow, but tonight you should do the following and check off each thing as you do it:

☐ Read the selection you have chosen three times.

☐ List the characters needed. Include the supernatural beings and the "voice of God" if needed.

☐ Write a description of the background you will use.

Remember that you will write or recite the memory challenge for a grade tomorrow.

Day 5

Today you should imagine that you are a writer for a movie production company. Your group will write a screen-play for the selection you have chosen. Begin by describing the background you need. Then you will need stage directions and dialog for your characters. Use the dialog from the Bible. Describe how you will present the angels. Describe the special effects you will use.

WRITING SCOREBOARD

1. Faithfulness to the Bible text. (25%)
2. Organization. (25%)
3. Creativity. (20%)
4. Following directions. (20%)
5. Mechanics: Grammar, spelling, etc. (10%)

On Your Own: Finish any writing you need to do on your "movie scene."

Day 6

Memory Challenge

"...Great and marvelous are your deeds, Lord God Almighty. Just and true are your ways, King of the ages. Who will not fear you, O Lord, and bring glory to your name? For you alone are holy. All nations will come and worship before you, for your righteous acts have been revealed." Rev. 15:3b-4

1. From the verses we have read, we clearly see that God is holy. Do you assume that Jesus is also holy? Why?

2. Today we move from looking at God's holiness in the Old Testament to the holiness of Jesus as seen in the New Testament. Read the following verses and write WHO declares Jesus to be holy (innocent, perfect, without fault.) Then write WHAT each person says about Him.

Reference	Who	What
(a) Mark 1:24		
(b) Matt. 27:3-4		
(c) Matt. 27:19		
(d) Luke 23:4 & 15		
(e) Heb. 4:15		
(f) Rev. 3:7 (See also Rev. 1:13.)		

On Your Own: 1. Read 2 Cor. 5:21. Thinking of the things we have studied in Bible class so far, why was it so important that Jesus be holy? Explain in your own words. Use at least four sentences.

2. Study the memory challenges. In three days you will be quizzed on all the verses from this quarter.

Day 7

1. There were a few days of fasting that the Jews observed every year. One of those was the Day of Atonement. Look up the Day of Atonement in a Bible dictionary and write what you find there.

2. Read Lev. 16:1-28. List ten of the things Aaron (and the high priests who came after him) had to do on the Day of Atonement. There are about fifteen things listed in these verses.

3. Why did they have to go to all this trouble?

4. Read Heb. 4:14-16 and 7:26-28.

(a) According to these verses, Jesus is our ______________________________ .

(b) According to verses 15 and 26, how is Jesus different from every other high priest? (List at least two ways.)

(c) Why is it important to us that Jesus was and is holy? (See vv. 26-28.)

(d) Re-read verses 15-16. It is also important to us that Jesus faced every temptation we face. Why? Write at least three sentences.

On Your Own: 1. According to Rev. 15, our memory challenge this week is a song. Read that chapter, then write down who sang that song and why they were singing.

2. For a similar song, read Ex. 15:11. Then read Ex. 15:1 to see who sang that song and why they were singing.

Day 8

Just like Moses in the past and saints in the future, we believers today like to sing songs to praise God. Sing or read these hymns then answer the questions.

1. "Holy, Holy, Holy"

(a) The second verse contains a reference to a Bible passage we have read. Which passage is it?

(b) The third verse contains another reference to a Bible story we have studied. Which story is it?

(c) Verses one and four are almost identical. How are they alike, and how are they different?

2. "Immortal, Invisible, God Only Wise"

(a) What does immortal mean?

(b) Why would light make it hard for us to see God?

(c) What scripture did we read that is a reference for the second line of the second stanza?

On Your Own:

Write your own hymn based on the following standards.

(a) It should be about God's holiness, but should also mention at least two of God's other attributes we have studied. (30%)

(b) It should follow the rhyme pattern ABCB or ABAB. (10%)

(c) It should contain at least two references to something in the Bible. (30%)

(d) It should be at least twelve lines (three stanzas) long. (20%)

(e) Grammar and spelling should be correct. (10%)

Note: Remember that you can reverse word order (ex.: Gracious Son of God is He) and shorten certain words (ex.: *o'er* for *over*; *e'en* for *even*) to help you gain the rhyme or rhythm you need. If you like, you may choose a tune that you know and make your words fit that tune.

Remember that in two days you will be tested on all the memory challenges you have had this quarter.

Day 9

But just as He who called you is holy, so be holy in all you do; 1 Peter 1:15

1. Share your hymn.

2. Read 2 Pet. 1:3-4.

(a) Who does the pronoun "His" refer to?

(b) What has Jesus given to "us" believers?

(c) "Everything" is a strong word. How is it possible that He could give us "everything we need for life and godliness"?

(d) Normally, we don't think of ourselves as holy. Yet in v. 4, Peter is telling us we can be holy. Which phrase(s) in v. 4 tells us that?

3. Knowing ourselves to be far from holy in the daily choices we make, how can we be holy? Read 1 John 1:8-9.

(a) What do you think "cleanse us from all unrighteousness" means?

(b) What do we have to do to receive this cleansing?

(c) What does *confess* mean?

4. From these verses in 1 John and 2 Peter, we can conclude that believers are holy when they have ______________________________

____.

5. How long does this holiness last?

Reflections: It is awesome to meditate on the holiness of God. It is even more awesome to think that we can "participate" in this holiness! Spend some time meditating on these two truths, then write your thoughts.

Remember, all your memory challenges are due tomorrow.

Day 10

1. Write or recite all the memory challenges from this quarter for a test grade.

2. Go over the study sheet to prepare for a test tomorrow.

On Your Own: Study for a test over Lesson 5.

Day 11

Take a test.

Lesson 5–Study Sheet

1. Define: Holy

   Exalted

   Scapegoat

   Immortal

   Confess

   Day of Atonement

2. List seven facts from the scene in which Isaiah saw God. (Isa. 6:1-7)

3. Write three ways in which cherubim and seraphs are different.

4. In Exodus 19, God warned Moses that the people should not step onto the mountain where God was talking to Moses. Why did God give such a strong warning about this?

5. We know we cannot see God, but in this lesson we have read of some tangible signs of His presence. List seven of them.

6. List five people who declared that Jesus was holy and tell what each one said about Him.

7. Why is it important to us today that Jesus lived a holy life?

8. According to 2 Pet., Jesus has given us ______________ we need for life and ______________.

Explain how this is possible.

9. Believers are holy when they have ____.

10. How long does this holiness last?

Reflections

Reflections

Reflections

Reflections

Reflections

Reflections

Reflections

Reflections

Reflections

Reflections

Reflections

Reflections

The Buddhist People

When you think of Buddhism, you probably think of a large statue of Buddha or of people doing yoga exercises. Orange robes, shaved heads, and worship of idols are common images of this religion. Today the majority of Buddhists, over 321 million, live in Asia in countries such as Tibet, Japan, China, Vietnam, and Thailand. However, there are over one and a half million in Europe and almost a million in North America.

The Buddhist People
Continued

Buddhists believe that men return to earth after death as different persons or as animals (reincarnation) based on their deeds while living. If they are good enough, they will finally earn their place in Nirvana (their idea of Heaven). Their good deeds include such things as following a knowledge of the truth, avoiding attachment to worldly things, and striving to free the mind from evil thoughts. While these are admirable goals, we know that man is not able to achieve goodness outside of Jesus Christ.

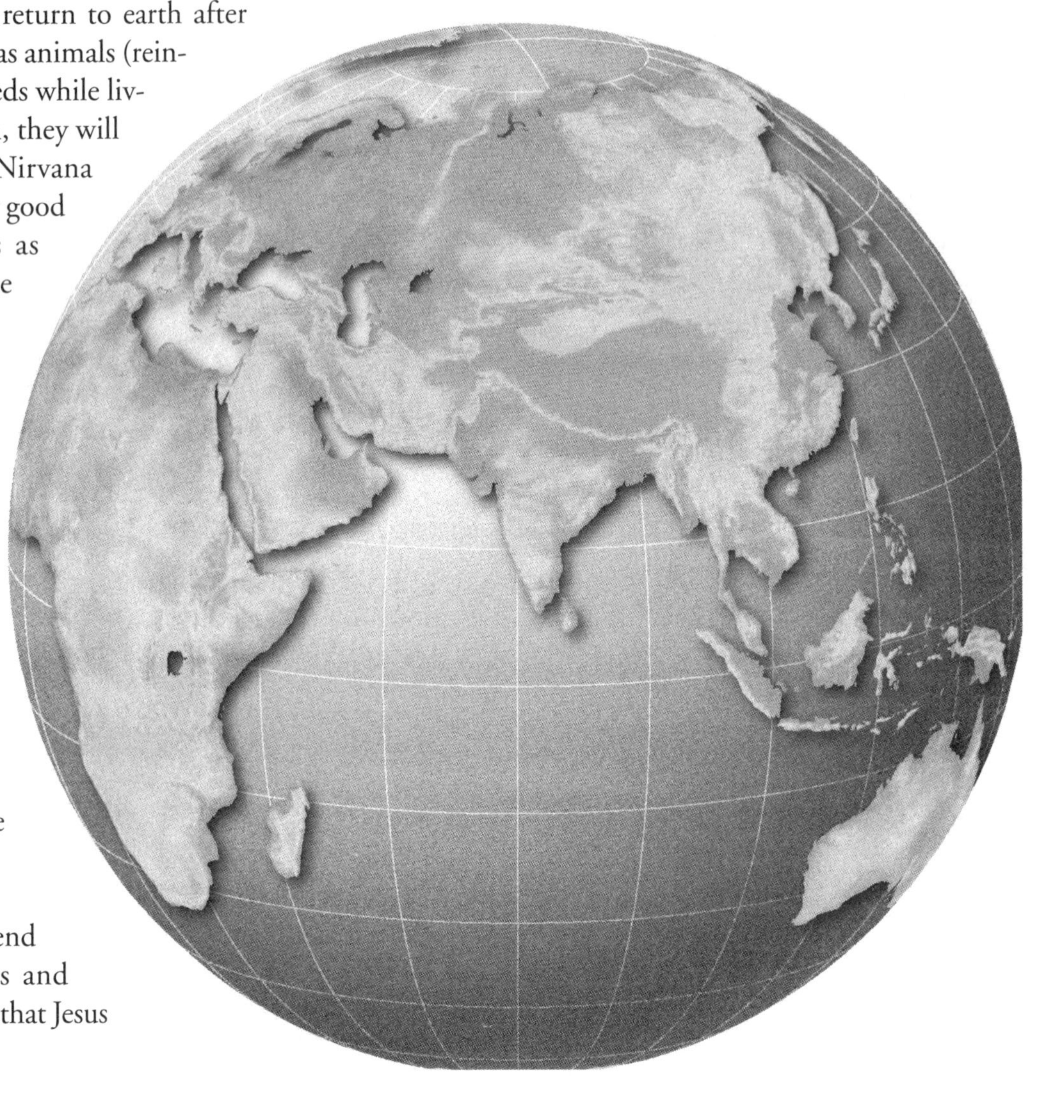

Buddhists seem to know they are not able to be good enough, too, as they live in fear that they have not done enough good things or made enough sacrifices.

How sad that Buddhists spend their lives worshiping idols and struggling to earn something that Jesus wants to give them as a gift.

Prayer Focus

Pray that God will open the hearts of Buddhists to receive Jesus–the living truth.

Pray for Christians who are willing to sacrifice to show love and kindness to Buddhists both overseas and here in the United States.

Pray that countries with large Buddhist populations would remain open to Christian missionaries.

Discovering God's Faithfulness

Lesson 6

Memory	*I will bow down toward your holy temple and will praise your name for your love and your faithfulness...* Ps. 138:2a *For the word of the LORD is right and true; he is faithful in all he does.* Ps. 33:4	Challenge

In the days of ancient Rome, a volcano erupted covering the city of Pompei with burning stones and lava. When the city was excavated in modern times, archeologists found the perfectly preserved bodies of a child and a dog. Even though the dog could have run to safety, it had chosen to remain with its young master. That is a picture of faithfulness here on earth.

1. Look up "faithful" in the dictionary and write out the definition.

A faithful person is a promise keeper. It is often difficult to keep our promises. Sometimes we forget. Sometimes it becomes inconvenient. Sometimes we make "pie-crust promises," –easily made, easily broken.

2. Is God a promise keeper? Make a list of five promises God made and kept in the Bible.

3. Look up the following verses and write them in your own words.

(a) 1 Cor. 1:9

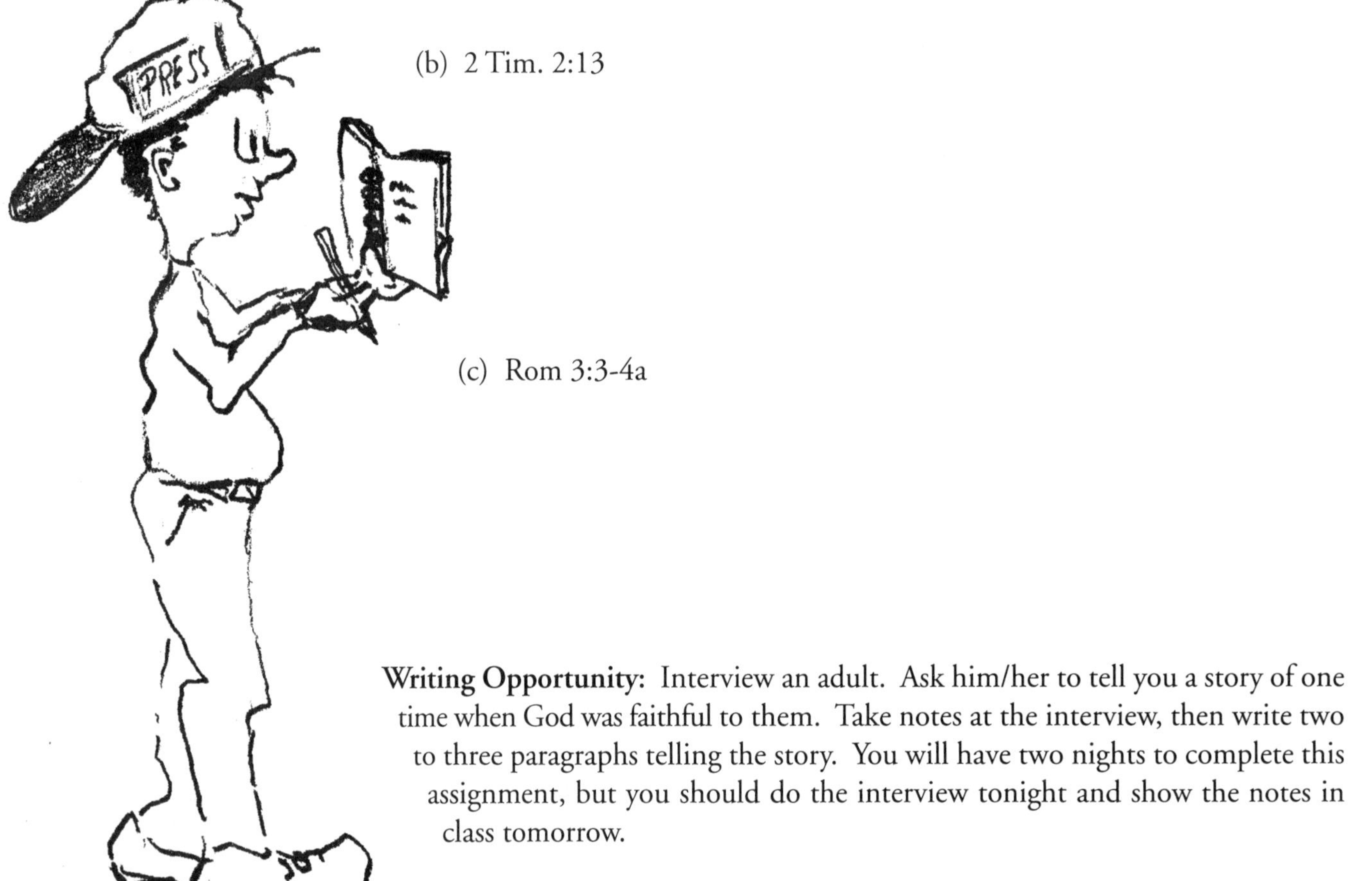

(b) 2 Tim. 2:13

(c) Rom 3:3-4a

Writing Opportunity: Interview an adult. Ask him/her to tell you a story of one time when God was faithful to them. Take notes at the interview, then write two to three paragraphs telling the story. You will have two nights to complete this assignment, but you should do the interview tonight and show the notes in class tomorrow.

WRITING SCOREBOARD

1. Completeness of story. (40%)
2. Organization. (20%)
3. Notes from the interview. (30%)
4. Mechanics: Grammar, spelling, etc. (10%)

Day 2

Read Ps. 107.

1. What phrase in v. 1 refers to God's faithfulness?

2. The first group of needy people is described in vv. 4-5. When they felt they were about to die, what did they do?

3. How did the Lord answer them?

4. The second group is described in verses _________ . Why were they having so many difficulties?

5. When they cried to the Lord for help, He____ .

6. Read vv. 17-18. These men were suffering because __________________________________.

7. How did they escape their troubles?

8. The final group of people is found in vv. 23-27. What was their problem?

9. What happened to them when they cried out to the Lord?

10. The point of Psalm 107 is that ____
.

11. We saw this same idea in one of the verses we read yesterday. Write that verse here, then explain it in your own words.

On Your Own: Finish your writing assignment.

Day 3

When I was in Jr. High, we girls loved to have secrets, especially secrets about boys we admired or had crushes on. After I solemnly promised I would never tell, one friend confided to me that she really, really liked Ronnie S. Even though I am now old, I still remember that within the hour I had broken my promise and told this secret to another friend. I think this incident is stuck in my memory because I felt so guilty about being a "promise breaker."

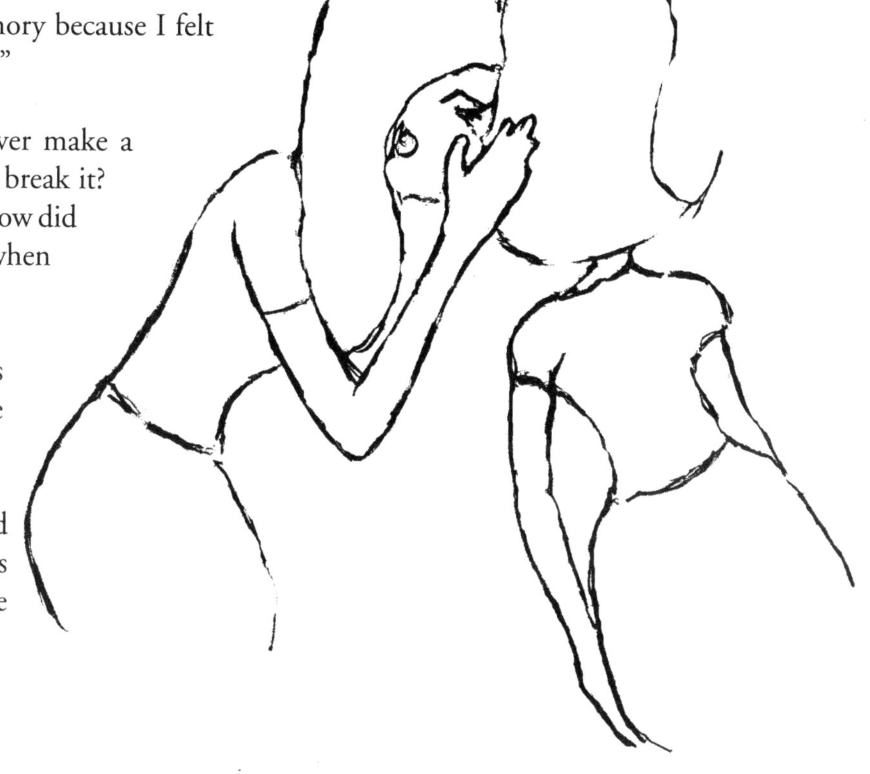

Are you a promise keeper? Did you ever make a promise and then forgetfully or willfully break it? Has someone broken a promise to you? How did that make you feel? Do you feel guilty when you break your word? Why or why not?

Our faithful God is a God of promise. As a matter of fact, the very name of our Bible speaks of a promise...

1. The word testament–as in the Old Testament and the New Testament–means *covenant.* Look up the word *covenant* in the dictionary and write out the definition.

God actually made covenants with several men (for example, Adam, Abram, and Moses) in Old Testament days. Let's examine the covenant God made with Abram (Abraham).

We can read God's first promises to Abram in Gen. 12 and 13. Among other things, God promised to make Abram into a great nation. However, in Gen. 15:8, Abram questioned God regarding that promise. Rather than being impatient with Abram, God desired to encourage him, so He went to great lengths to formalize the convenant.

2. Read Gen. 15:1-6.

(a) According to vv. 1-3, what reason did Abram have to be discouraged?

(b) What picture did God show Abram as a simile for Abram's descendents?

(c) According to v. 6, Abram believed God, and God ______________________________.

(d) Because of v. 6, Paul could later say of Abraham that he was justified by ______________.

However, Abram was like us in that he wanted some proof of God's intentions. In v. 8 he asked God, "How can I be sure that I will inherit the land you have promised me?"

On Your Own: Read Gen. 15:7-17. In vv. 9-12 and 17 of Gen. 15, we read of the physical pledge God made to prove to Abram that He would keep His word. Draw a diagram or a picture showing the details of that pledge. Label the items used for the sacrifice. Include Abram in your picture.

Day 4

Read Gen. 15:12-21.

1. In the chart below, write down the things God promised Abram according to the verses listed.

Verse	Promise
v. 13	
v. 14	
v. 15	
v. 16	
v. 18	

2. According to chapter 15, what did God ask of Abram in return for all these blessings?

On Your Own: Read Gen. 17:16-22 and answer the following questions.

1. What special promise did God make to Sarah as a part of this covenant?

2. Abraham reacted to that promise by ______________________

______________________________________.

3. How long had Abraham been waiting for the descendents God had promised him? (See Gen. 12:1-4.)

____.

4. It is easy for us to think that Abraham was foolish to laugh at God, but we need to remember that at this point Abraham really did not know God very well. He thought God's promise could not be fulfilled because

____.

5. God even told Abraham and Sarah what to name the child. His name would be ____________________,

which means ________________________, because of the joy he would bring this couple in their old age.

6. When was Sarah going to have the baby?

7. Who was Ishmael, and what was going to happen to him?

8. Study the memory challenge. It is due tomorrow.

Day 5

1. Write or recite the memory challenge.

2. Enjoy the guest speaker.

On Your Own: 1. Read the promise God made to Abraham in Gen. 18:18. Write that promise in your own words. Tell how you think God intended to fulfill that promise.

2. Read Acts 3:25. Write a sentence telling how this scripture is related to the one in Gen. 18.

Day 6

For to us a child is born, to us a son is given, and the government will be on his shoulders. And he will be called Wonderful Counselor, Mighty God, Everlasting Father, Prince of Peace. Isa. 9:6

1. Read Jer. 31:31-34.

(a) In v. 33, God promises to put His law in the

____

and ____________________ of His people.

(b) In v. 34, He says that all His people will __________.

(c) How is this possible?

Very early in the Old Testament we read God's first promise of a Messiah.

2. Read Gen. 3:13-15. What do you think God is promising in v. 15?

3. Listen to these verses.

Isa. 7:14; Micah 5:2; Hosea 11:1; Isa. 9:7; Zec. 9:9-10; Jer. 23:5-6.

Now listen to them again and underline all the words in each verse that refer to Jesus.

On Your Own: 1. Read Jer. 31:15 and Hosea 11:1. Remembering what you know of the Christmas story, what two events do you think these scriptures foretell?

2. Write some references to show where these events are found in the New Testament.

Keep your handouts–you will need them in class tomorrow.

Day 7

Yesterday you listened to several prophecies which were also God's promises regarding the New Covenant. Today you'll take a closer look at those promises.

In the chart below, do the following:
(a) After each reference, write two or three key words to tell what is being predicted. (If you have the handout from yesterday, you will not have to look these up.)

(b) At the bottom of the chart are New Testament references {section (c)} which tell of the fulfillment of the promises given in the Old Testament. Look up these references and match them with the appropriate promise.

OT Ref.	Key Words (Prediction)	NT References (from section c)
1. Is. 7:14		
2. Micah 5:2		
3. Hosea 11:1		
4. Is. 9:7		
5. Zec. 9:9-10		
6. Jer. 23:5-6		

(c) Luke 3:31-34; Matt. 2:1; Matt. 1:18-24; Matt. 1:1-17; Matt. 1:6; Matt. 21:2, 6-7; Matt. 2:14.

Reflections: Write a paragraph of at least five sentences explaining why it is important to you that so many details of Jesus' birth were predicted in Old Testament days.

Share and discuss your reflections.

1. Read Josh. 21:45 and Num. 23:19.

Both of these verses are making the same point; what is it?

2. Read the scriptures assigned to your group. Using a large poster board and a bright marker, write the promises God has given us in these verses.

Group I

2 Tim 1:1; Eph. 1:13; 2 Cor. 6:18; Titus 1:2

Group II

Heb. 8:12; Gal. 3:18; James 1:12; Rom. 1:1-2

Group III

1 John 1:9; Acts 13:22-23; 1 John 2:25; Heb. 8:10

On Your Own: Study all the memory challenge verses for this lesson. They will be due in two days.

Day 9

1. Share the promises from your poster.

2. What reason do we have to believe that these promises will be kept?

3. Which of God's attributes that we have studied tell us He is *able* to keep His promises?

4. Which of God's attributes that we have studied tell us He *desires* to keep His promises?

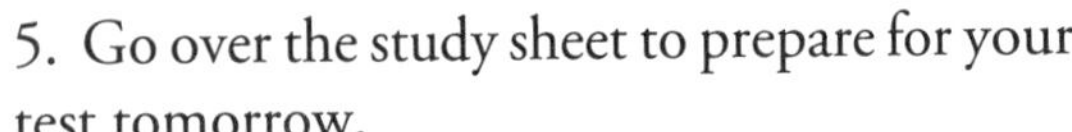

5. Go over the study sheet to prepare for your test tomorrow.

On Your Own: Study for the Lesson 6 test, including the memory challenge verses.

Day 10

Take a test.

Lesson 6–Study Sheet

1. Define: Faithful

   Covenant

2. Write a short paragraph explaining the main point of Ps. 107. Include specific references to the Psalm to support your ideas.

3. Describe the scene in which God confirmed His covenant with Abram. Include at least seven specific details.

4. List five of the things God promised Abram.

5. How old were Abram and Sarah when Isaac was born?

6. Tell what Abram named his son and why he chose that name.

7. List five promises God makes to believers that you learned about in your study.

8. Match the following statements with their references.

____ Isa. 7:14	a. Jesus will be taken to Egypt.
____ Micah 5:2	b. The king of Israel will come riding on a donkey.
____ Hosea 11:1	c. A virgin will have a baby boy and will name him Immanuel.
____ Isa. 9:7	d. God will raise up a king from David's line; He will bring justice.
____ Zec. 9:9-10	e. The Messiah will come from David; He will reign over much territory forever, in peace.
____ Jer. 23:5-6	f. The Messiah will be born in Bethlehem.

Reflections

Reflections

Reflections

Reflections

Reflections

Reflections

Reflections

The Tribal People

There are thousands of different tribal groups scattered throughout the world. From China to Siberia to Indonesia, each group has a distinct language, culture, and religious belief. Yet, they have one thing in common–their animistic beliefs make them slaves to evil practices and to fear of punishment by their gods.

The Tribal People
Continued

Some tribes in Africa have over 1,000,000 members, and some in Papua New Guinea have fewer than 500. Some tribal people still roam the jungles of South America wearing little clothing and eating what they can find. Others in Africa include the well educated and rulers of the country. Many tribal people live constantly ready for war as they are historical enemies with those who live near them.

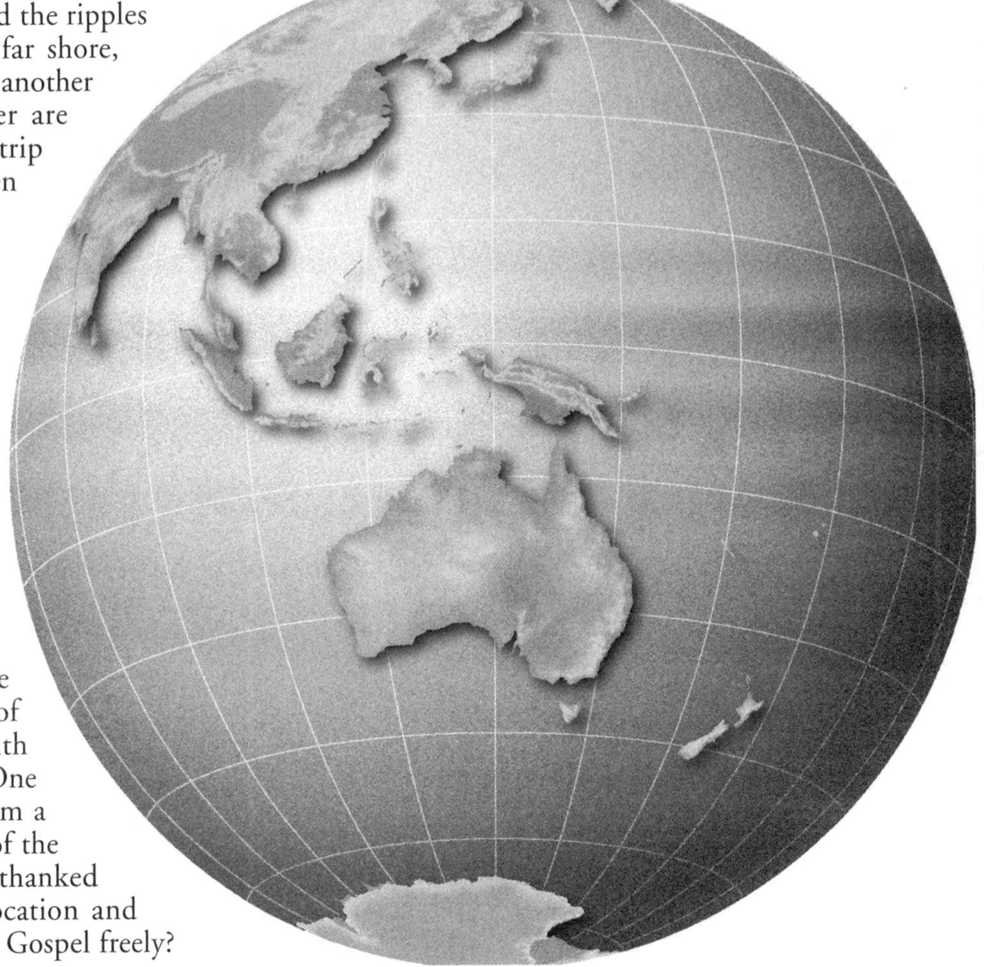

If a stone splashes into a pond and the ripples spread across the surface to the far shore, those ripples will have no effect on another pond if the two bodies of water are separated by even a very narrow strip of land. In the same manner, when the Gospel penetrates one culture and new believers form a church, that doesn't mean that the "good news" will necessarily spread into another nearby tribal group. This means that usually missionaries trained in cross-cultural ministry will have to go live with the people and learn their language, their culture, and their beliefs in order to share Christ in a meaningful, life-changing way.

Do you think it's a waste of time when a missionary spends years of his or her life to reach a tribe with only a few hundred people in it? One missionary said, "It wouldn't seem a waste if I had been born as one of the few hundred." Have you ever thanked God that you were born in a location and culture where you could hear the Gospel freely?

One saved tribal man in Papua New Guinea told the missionary, "It was just like I lived in darkness, but now I see the light." Indeed, Jesus is the light of the world. Who will take that light to tribal people?

Prayer Focus

For Christians who love Jesus enough to sacrifice their comfort and live among tribal people so they can effectively share the gospel.

For official permission for missionaries to enter or stay in countries to work with the tribes.

For safety and boldness for tribal Christians who go out to witness to their friends or to other tribes.

Discovering God's Justice

Lesson

Memory Challenge

Your arm is endued with power; your hand is strong, your right hand exalted. Righteousness and justice are the foundation of your throne; love and faithfulness go before you. Ps. 89:13-14.

No matter how hard you try, you cannot see all the facets of a prism at once. That's the way it is when we try to understand the justice of God. It is hard for us to grasp the true meaning of God's justice. His justice begins with His holiness. It is also an essential part of His righteousness.

Zephaniah the prophet wrote, "But the Lord is there within the city, and *he does no wrong.* Day by day his justice is more evident..." *(Living Bible Paraphrase)*

1. Think carefully about this statement: everything God does agrees with His own standards. What does that mean to you?

Does it mean all His actions are perfect and just? When God judges our sin according to His holiness–that is just. When He allows us to suffer the consequences of our own sinful actions, however painful those consequences may be–that is just–for He cannot be anything else.

2. Define justice.

(a) Write your own definition.

(b) Write a dictionary definition.

(c) Fill in the blanks as your teacher reads the following Bible definitions:

(1) ______________ for violating God's ______________ ______________.

(2) The ______________ ______________ that God uses to measure our ______________.

(3) God's ______________ of ______________ for his children.

On Your Own: Write some of the major differences between the dictionary definition of justice and the biblical ones. Study the memory challenge.

Day 2

The first story we are going to study has to do with the first biblical definition of justice. It's a story that comes from the time of the judges. Do you remember Gideon?

This story begins at the end of Gideon's life. Listen and fill in the answers to the questions as your teacher reads the first part of the story (Judges 8:29-9:6) in a modern language translation. You will notice that Gideon had another name–Jerubbaal.

If you need more thinking time on a question, skip it and then go back to it once your teacher has finished reading.

1. Gideon had _________ son(s) in his palace from his wives and concubines.

2. He had ________ son(s) by a concubine in Shechem.

Note: Shechem had been a town, or village, since the days of Jacob (Gen. 33:18). It was located to the west of the Jordan River. The ruins of Shechem have been discovered by archeologists.

3. If we look back at the verses at the end of Judges 8, we find that after the death of Gideon, Israel turned _______

____.

4. Therefore, in a way, the rule of Abimelech over Israel shows God's ________________________________

against them because they violated ________________________________ . (vv. 33-35)

5. Which of the three biblical definitions of God's justice does this represent?

6. When Abimelech wanted to fight against his half-brothers, who did he choose to help him?

7. Why do you think they were willing to do this?

8. Abimelech and his followers killed _________________ of Gideon's sons.

9. What do you think the phrase "on one stone" means?

10. Who was Jotham?

11. How do you think Jotham was feeling at this point? Why?

On Your Own: Read the parable of Jotham in Judges 7-15. Draw a cartoon strip to illustrate this parable. Use one frame for each type of tree Jotham talks about. *(You may choose to use only five of the boxes if you prefer.)*

Write a brief explanation of this parable.

Day 3

In the second part of chapter 9, we see God's divine justice rendered to Abimelech and his followers. Read vv. 17-57.

1. How many years have passed?

2. According to v. 23, God stirred up the people so they

____.

3. Why do you think God did this? (See v. 24.)

4. God also raised up a newcomer to Shechem, named __________________, who incited the men of Shechem

against ______________________________________.

5. Who is Zebul?

6. Describe the plan Abimelech plotted against Gaal and his followers.

7. According to verse 45, what four things did Abimelech do to the city and the people of Shechem?

8. Apparently there was a small settlement nearby where some of the leaders of Shechem hid in a fort or a tower. What did Abimelech do about that problem?

9. How does what happened to these men from Shechem reflect Jotham's curse?

10. What is your estimation of Abimelech as a man?

11. How was Abimelech finally killed?

12. There is a kind of justice in the fact that Abimelech was mortally wounded with a stone. Explain how that seems an especially fit ending for him.

Reflections: Meditate on God's retribution as a part of His justice. Write a paragraph of at least seven sentences telling what this means to you.

Day 4

What do you think God wants you to learn from the story of Abimelech? Write down at least three things you learned.

On Your Own: Tomorrow you will write or recite your memory challenges for a grade.

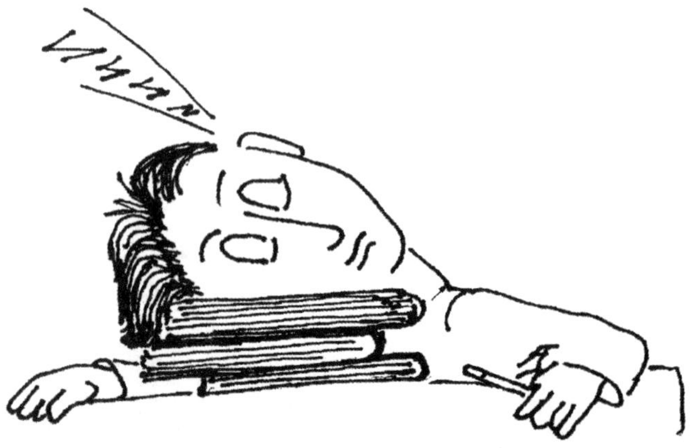

Day 5

Since God is our judge, it is important to consider what standards He uses. A few days ago, we learned that God's actions always agree with His own standards. We can't meet the standards God has set for Himself, but God has given us standards by which to judge our own actions.

1. What moral standards does God use to judge our actions?

2. Read Ps. 51:3-4. When we lie, steal, gossip, are impatient or unloving, or disobey our parents, who are we sinning against?

3. How was God justified in judging David?

4. How is He justified in judging us?

The story of King David and his sin with Bathsheba illustrates another facet of God's justice–the moral standards that God uses to measure our actions.

5. Which of the Ten Commandments did David violate, and how?

Commandment	David's Sin
(a)	
(b)	
(c)	
(d)	

6. David fooled many people with his maneuvers. Did he fool God?

7. Write out the verse that proves your answer.

Reflections: Think of a time when you tried to fool God in order to cover up your sin. Write seven to ten sentences about what happened.

Day 6

Memory Challenge

For I know my transgressions, and my sin is always before me. Against you, you only, have I sinned and done what is evil in your sight, so that you are proved right when you speak and justified when you judge. Ps. 51:3-4

Yesterday we agreed that David was not able to fool God. Today we will read about how God dealt with David's sin.

1. Read 2 Sam. 12:1-3. Who was Nathan?

2. Draw two pictures to illustrate the two men in Nathan's parable.

3. Read v. 4. Write all the descriptive words you can think of that fit the rich man and/or his actions.

4. Who do you think the characters in Nathan's parable represent?

(a) The poor man –

(b) His ewe lamb –

(c) The rich man –

5. Read vv. 5-7. How did David feel about the rich man in the parable?

6. How do you think David felt when Nathan said, "You are the rich man."?

WRITING SCOREBOARD

1. Illustration of the truth chosen: Does the story give a good "picture" of the truth you wish to present? (50%)

2. Creativity in the use of characters: Are the characters fitting to the story, interesting, and uniquely your own? (20%)

3. Organization: Does the story have a beginning, a middle, and a conclusion? (20%)

4. Mechanics: Grammar, spelling, etc. (10%)

Writing Opportunity: Parables are often used to help the listener grasp an idea that is difficult to understand. This is the second parable we have read in this lesson. Over the next two nights, you will write your own parable. Choose the truth that you want to illustrate and write it at the top of your paper. Choose people or plants to represent your characters. Be sure the parable is clear enough that others in the class will understand it.

Day 7

To find out about God's hand of justice toward David, read 2 Sam. 12: 7-13. Nathan charged David with violating each of the standards we listed in the chart on Day 5.

1. List the verses from Nathan's speech that identify each moral standard David broke.

(a) Covetousness –

(b) Adultery –

(c) Murder –

2. God's justice "fits the crime." What punishment did Nathan predict for each violation?

(a) For murder –

(b) For adultery –

(c) For lying –

3. Why didn't God either kill David or remove him from his position as King? (v. 13)

On Your Own: Finish your parable.

Day 8

Read your parable to the class.

To see the true state of David's heart after Nathan's accusations, read Ps. 51. Then answer the following questions.

1. What excuse did David make for his sin?

2. Who did David blame for his sin?

3. From Ps. 51, write five phrases that show us David deeply repented from his sin.

4. According to David, what sacrifice is most pleasing to God?

5. What do you think a "broken spirit" is?

6. What do you think a "contrite heart" is?

Reflections: What does David's story tell you about God's justice? Write at least five sentences.

Remember to practice your memory challenges. They will be due in two days.

Day 9

1. Share your On Your Own answers and discuss them in class.

2. Fill in the blanks:

(a) God's justice demands that sin has____________________________.

(b) God's mercy provides ____________________ for sin when we ______________________________________ .

(c) Does forgiveness remove the consequences of sin? ____________________________.

(d) Use an illustration from David's life to support your answer to (c).

3. For each of David's violations of God's moral standards, Nathan prophesied regarding the punishment. Do you think Nathan's prophecies all came true? ___________

Look up the following verses and write what happened.

Nathan's Prophecy	Actual Event
(a) The baby would die. (2 Sam. 12:18).	
(b) The sword would not depart from David's house (2 Sam. 13:23-29, 2 Sam 18:9-14, 1 Kings 2:23-25).	
(c) David's wives would be taken by another (2 Sam. 16:21-22).	
(d) The event above would happen in public (2 Sam. 16:21-22).	

Reflections: God's justice is a part of His character. His love and mercy are also a part of His character. One of these characteristics does not cancel out the other. Sin must come under God's judgment, and God's justice demands that sin be punished! Write a paragraph of at least five sentences explaining what this fact means to you.

Remember to study your memory challenges. They are due tomorrow.

Day 10

1. Write or recite your memory challenges.
2. Watch a video.

Day 11

1. Share your paragraphs from Day 9 if you choose.

2. Read John 8:1-8.

(a) Imagine this scene in your head.

(b) Who suddenly appears in the midst of the crowd?

(c) The men say they are going to stone the woman. What does this mean?

(d) They are legally correct because ______________ gave them this law.

(e) Why do they have to ask Jesus their question more than once?

(f) How many times do you think they asked?

(g) When Jesus finally answers them, He says ____.

3. What does Jesus' statement have to do with justice?

4. Of all the people in that crowd, who had the right to render justice to this woman? ____________
Why?

5. Read verses 9-11.

(a) Because Jesus has the authority to give justice, He is also able to justly choose to forgive the woman. How do we know He forgave her?

(b) What commandment did Jesus give the woman?

(c) Do you think she obeyed this commandment? ______ Give a reason for your answer.

On Your Own:
1. This woman's sin was similar to David's, yet her treatment was different. Imagine that you are the judge listening to these two cases. List at least three ways the woman's case was different than David's.

2. What do you think Jesus wrote on the ground? Give good reasons for your answer.

3. Which men do you think left first? Give good reasons for your answer.

4. **After** you have answered questions 2 and 3, interview two *adults* and ask them these questions. Write down their answers.

Day 12

Review and ponder.

1. We have learned that sin has ______________________________.

2. According to Genesis 2:17, God told Adam and Eve that if they ate of the forbidden fruit they would ______ __________ .

3. Since they did not "die" immediately, we know that God did not mean ____________________________ death, but ____________________________ death.

4. Read Rom. 6:23.

(a) According to Rom. 6:23, the wages of sin is ______________________.

(b) Which kind of death do you think Paul meant?

(c) Why do you think that?

5. Read Ps. 5:15 and 45:6-7. How does God feel about sin?

6. Explain why God has to sentence the sinner to death.

Writing Opportunity: Read Rom. 4:24-25, 5:8, and 8:32. Think about these verses and all we have studied in this unit. Write a paragraph (of at least ten sentences) explaining why Jesus had to die on the cross. Include in your paragraph an explanation of at least one of these verses to help support your ideas.

WRITING SCOREBOARD

1. Explanation: Is it clear? Is it logical? (50%)
2. Following directions. (20%)
3. Organization. (20%)
4. Mechanics: Grammar, spelling, etc. (10%)

Day 13

Share your paragraph.

Answer the questions on the study sheet.

On Your Own: Study for a test over Lesson 7.

Day 14

Take a test over Lesson 7.

Lesson 7–Study Sheet

1. Define: Justice

   Contrite

2. Identify each of the following people in one or two sentences.

(a) Gideon

(b) Jotham

(c) Abimelech

(d) Uriah

(e) Nathan

3. Why did Jotham curse the men of Shechem?

4. How was his curse fulfilled?

5. Write down three things you learned from the story of Abimelech.

6. How was God justified in judging David?

7. What method did Nathan use to open David's eyes to his sin?

8. Does forgiveness remove the consequences of sin? Use an illustration from David's life to support your answer.

9. What commandment did Jesus give to the adulterous woman who was almost stoned?

10. How does God feel about sin?

11. Explain in a few sentences why Jesus had to die on the cross. Give some scripture references to support your ideas.

Reflections

Reflections

Reflections

Reflections

Reflections

Reflections

The People in Your Neighborhood

Ethnic peoples, distant lands, unusual customs: all are intriguing and exciting, but the people next door or across the street need Christ, too. Most of us can't pack up and go off to Africa, Indonesia, or China. However, we can look for opportunities to witness to the people we meet every day.

Sometimes the bus driver who smiles and greets you every morning, the classmate who sits next to you, the folks you baby-sit for, even the friend who shares your lunch table and your secrets is a person who is hurting and needy. All people, even if they have always lived in America and have gone to church many times, need to have a personal faith in Jesus Christ.

Not all missionaries live overseas. Missionaries are also people–like you–who introduce Jesus to the people next door. In your neighborhood, there may be Hindus, Muslims, Buddhists, or just ordinary people like you only they are lost and lonely without a Savior. Jesus gives you the privilege of witnessing about Him to those you meet each day.

The People in Your Neighborhood
Continued

Note: This particular Prayer Focus is different than the others in that you can pray for these people specifically, by name.

Prayer Focus

That God would show you if there is an unsaved person that you meet every day.

That God would show you opportunities to demonstrate love and kindness to your neighbors as a first step in sharing Christ with them.

That God would give you wisdom and boldness to talk to your friends and neighbors about Him.

That God would draw the people in your neighborhood to Himself.

Discovering God's Mercy

Lesson 8

Memory

Because of the LORD's great love we are not consumed, for his compassions never fail. They are new every morning; great is your faithfulness. Lam. 3:22-23

Challenge

Can you remember half-waking in the night to realize that your mother was quietly covering you with the blanket you had kicked onto the floor? How cozy to snuggle under that blanket, warmed by its cover, but also warmed by your mother's love. In the same way, God covers us with His mercy. According to this verse from Lamentations, He covers us *every day*.

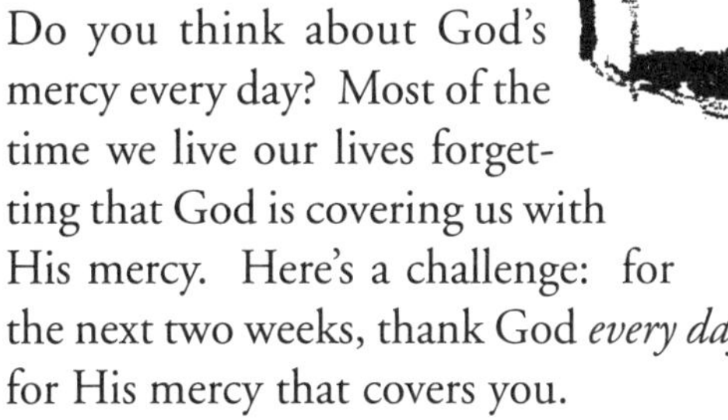

Do you think about God's mercy every day? Most of the time we live our lives forgetting that God is covering us with His mercy. Here's a challenge: for the next two weeks, thank God *every day* for His mercy that covers you.

1. Define *mercy.*

2. Make a list of examples of mercy you remember from the Bible. Your examples could come from the Old Testament or the New; they could be examples of God's mercy or mercy shown by one person to another. When you have five examples listed, raise your hand.

3. Share your examples with the class.

4. Can you think of a time when a person showed mercy to you? What about a time when you showed mercy to another person? List at least two of these incidents.

5. Our acts of mercy are small compared to God's, yet we know that God is pleased when we show mercy to others. How do we know this?

Writing Opportunity: This week you are going to write a short story! Look back at question #4. Choose one of the incidents you listed (or another one you can think of). Write a short story about what happened. You will have four nights to write this story. Before class tomorrow, list

☛ (a) the incident you chose,

☛ (b) the setting,

☛ (c) the characters who will appear in your story.

Also write at least the first half-page of your rough draft.

Schedule for the story:
Tonight: see above.

Tomorrow night: you should write one to two more pages.

The third night: finish your rough draft.

Final night: polish and do any rewriting; have the story ready to turn in.

WRITING SCOREBOARD

1. Organization of plot: Does it have a beginning? Does it move along smoothly? Does it show a realistic problem and a solution to the problem? 25%

2. Characters: Do the people in the story speak and act like real people? 25%

3. Theme: Does the story clearly show an act of mercy? 25%

4. Creativity: Is the language lively and interesting? 15%

5. Mechanics: Grammar, spelling, etc. 10%

Day 2

Enjoy a guest speaker.

On Your Own: Follow the writing schedule from Day 1. Study the memory challenge.

Day 3

Read 2 Sam. 4:4 and chapter 9.

1. What was Mephibosheth's handicap, and how did he receive it?

2. Mephibosheth's grandfather was ______________ and his father was ______________________________.

3. Why did David want to show mercy (kindness) to Mephibosheth?

4. Remember how Saul had treated David. What do you think Mephibosheth might have expected from David?

5. When Mephibosheth first saw David, he ______________________________.

6. When David was kind to Mephibosheth, the lame man referred to himself as a ______________.

7. Why do you think he said that?

8. Make a list of some of the kindnesses David showed to Mephibosheth.

On Your Own: Follow the writing schedule from Day 1. Study the memory challenge. Your memory challenge is due the day after tomorrow.

Day 4

Many of the Old Testament happenings are a picture to help us understand the gospel more clearly. The story of Mephibosheth is such a story.

1. Who do you think King David could represent in this story? Why?

2. Who do you think Mephibosheth could represent? Why?

3. In the following blanks, list some ways Mephibosheth is like us.

(a) Before David called him to the palace, he was ________________. Before we were saved, we were ________________________.

(b) Mephibosheth gained his new life, **not** because of anything ______________________. We gain salvation **not** because of anything ______________________.

(c) Mephibosheth was saved by the ____________ of David. We are saved by the ____________ of God.

(d) For the rest of his life, Mephibosheth lived ____. For all eternity, we will live ____________________.

4. From this comparison, we see that in this story, King David is an example of God's ________________.

5. As King David sought Mephibosheth, found him and brought him to the palace, so our merciful God _ _ _ _ _ _ us even when we were sinners, He _ _ _ _ _ us and _ _ _ _ _ _ _ _ us to Himself.

On Your Own: Your short stories are due tomorrow. You should know your memory challenge by tomorrow.

Day 5

1. Background: In 445 BC, Nehemiah was allowed to take some of the Israelites from exile in ____________ ______________________________________and return to ___________. His objective was to rebuild the _____________________________, and to reestablish Jewish life in this sacred city.

As we begin reading in Neh. 9, the walls had been rebuilt, and the people had gathered together to worship God. In vv. 1-15, one of the Levites recounted the history of the Israelites beginning with Abraham. In v. 16, he began the confession of their sins in the journey from Egypt to the Promised Land.

Read Neh. 9:22-31.

2. In vv. 22-26, we read a description of the Israelites' conquest of the ______________________________ .

3. In these verses, the speaker gives all the credit and praise to _______________________________ .

4. Read v. 25 again and list some of the good things God gave the Jews.

5. How would you expect the Israelites to act after receiving all these blessings from God?

6. How did they actually react?

7. How did God discipline the Israelites?

8. Draw a line from each of the words below to the action that followed. Use arrows to show the direction of the action.

DISCIPLINE	REPENTANCE
RESTORATION	REBELLION

9. How many times was this pattern repeated in the lives of the Israelites?

What verse tells you this?

10. What do we learn about God in Neh. 9:31?

11. What evidence supports this description of God?

Reflections: Read the following poem. In your journal, write a paragraph explaining the meaning of this poem. Then tell what it means to you personally.

I sought the Lord, and afterward I knew,
He moved my soul, to seek Him seeking me.
It was not I who found, oh, Savior, true.
No, I was found by Thee.
–author unknown

Day 6

He has showed you, O man, what is good. And what does the LORD require of you? To act justly and to love mercy and to walk humbly with your God. Micah 6:8

One favorite story about Jesus' mercy has to do with Simon Peter.

1. Do you remember what Peter did when Jesus was on trial?

2. How many times did Peter deny Jesus?

3. How did he feel after his denial? (See Matt. 26:75.)

4. Read John 21:1-17.

(a) What is the setting of this story?

(b) List the main characters.

(c) What did Jesus do after their supper?

(d) How many times did He question Peter?

(e) Each time Peter gave the same answer. How do you think Peter was feeling by the the final question?

(f) What evidence do you have for this opinion?

5. There are many significant ideas in this passage, but we are focusing primarily on Jesus' mercy toward Peter. Explain how Jesus showed His mercy to Peter in a special way by His actions here.

6. In the NIV translation, you will see that each time Jesus answered Peter in a slightly different way. Peter had a great deal of time to think about what Jesus meant by His answers. What do you think He meant?

7. Did Peter obey Jesus' commands? How do you know?

On Your Own: Using your concordance, locate a Psalm which talks about God's mercy (kindness, compassion). Choose eight to fifteen verses (your teacher may assign a specific number) from the Psalm. Write at least five sentences telling what these verses mean to you, then practice reading them aloud at least three times. Read them aloud to the class tomorrow. Be prepared to explain any of the verses when asked about what they mean, as well as what they mean to you.

Day 7

Read the Psalm you have prepared, then share what it means to you.

On Your Own: Study your memory challenges from the last four weeks. They will be due on the test day.

Day 8

Field trip!

Reflections: Write seven to eleven sentences telling your thoughts about the field trip.

Day 9

Answer the questions on the study sheet to help prepare for the test tomorow.

On Your Own: Study for the test on Lesson 8.

Day 10

Take a test.

Lesson 8–Study Sheet

1. Define: Mercy

   Consumed

   Compassion

2. List five examples of God's mercy from Bible stories (other than the stories we studied in class).

3. Mephibosheth's grandfather was ________________________; his father was ________________________.

4. Mephibosheth was handicapped because ____.

5. List two of the kindnesses David showed to Mephibosheth.

6. In this Bible story, David could represent ____________ because ____________________________.

7. Mephibosheth could represent ________________ because ____________________________.

8. In 445 BC, Nehemiah lived in _____________________ , but he wanted to go to ________________ in order to ____.

9. When the Israelites reached the Promised Land, God gave them many good gifts. List four of these.

10. Write in order the four words that show the pattern of the Israelites' actions and God's actions as seen in Nehemiah.

11. How many times did God forgive the Israelites?

12. Why did He forgive them so many times?

13. _____________ times Jesus asked Peter, "________ ___________ ___________ _______?"

14. Write a brief paragraph telling why you think Jesus asked Peter this same question several times.

15. Write a brief paragraph explaining one thing you learned from the field trip.

Reflections

Reflections

Reflections

Reflections

Reflections

Reflections

Reflections

Summary Lesson

"Let not the wise man boast of his wisdom or the strong man boast of his strength or the rich man boast of his riches, but let him who boasts boast about this: that he understands and knows me, that I am the Lord, who exercises kindness, justice, and righteousness on earth, for in these I delight," declares the Lord. Jer. 9:23-24

When we began this semester, our goal was to understand God better–who He is, what His characteristics are, and how knowing Him affects the way we live.

Today we want to look back over the semester to see if we achieved that goal. Read the following questions and spend five minutes thinking about your answers. Then you will have an opportunity to share in class.

1. What was the most important thing you learned about God from these lessons?

2. How does that knowledge affect the way you live?

After the discussion, spend time praying and thanking God for the specific things He has taught you during this study.

Discovering Who I Am In Christ, (Book 2)
7th, 8th, or 9th Grade Bible Curriculum
Jan L. Harris, Howard & Bonnie Lisech,

If you enjoyed *Discovering Our Amazing God* (Book 1) the second in this exciting curriculum series will help you understand your identity in Christ. These life changing principles are the focus of *Discovering Who I Am In Christ* (Book 2). It also has line drawings, and suggested activities intermingled with inductive Bible study to challenge and encourage you in your Christian walk. The Teacher's Guide and Student Workbook are similar in layout and function as *Discovering Our Amazing God.* Each lesson also introduces an unreached people group to help you to learn about the peoples of our world. Ask your parent or home school teacher to check it out at ***www.DeeperRoots.com*** where they can order FREE pdf sample pages from the teacher's guide.

211DCHSTG Home School (Teacher's Guide)...$28.95

212DCHSSW Home School (Student Workbook) ...$19.95

Discovering Christ–like Habits, (Book3)
7th, 8th, or 9th Grade Bible Curriculum
Jan L. Harris, Howard & Bonnie Lisech,

Discovering Christ–like Habits is the third book in our DISCOVERING... series, and it is designed to help you change the patterns of your life. This book provides not only a deeper understanding of Christian habits, but also helps you to learn to practice disciplines like prayer, worship, obeying from your will, Bible study, etc. The lessons combine inductive Bible studies with plenty of hands-on activities, writing stories, interviewing family members, planning and acting out Bible dramas, and taking a field trip. You will learn practical, godly habits while deepening your relationship with Jesus. Each lesson also introduces an unreached people group to help you understand the peoples of our world. Ask your parent or home school teacher to check it out at ***www.DeeperRoots.com*** where they can order FREE pdf sample pages from the teacher's guide.

221DHHSTG Home School (Teacher's Guide)...$28.95

222DHHSSW Home School (Student Workbook) ...$19.95

Discovering A Christ–Like Character, (Book 4)
7th, 8th, or 9th Grade Bible Curriculum
Jan L. Harris, Howard & Bonnie Lisech,

Discovering A Christ–Like Character is the final book in the DISCOVERING... series. It uses Bible accounts of Christ's life to challenge you to a lifetime of following His example. As you focus on the character of Jesus, such as His compassion, mercy, forgiveness, and patience, you will be drawn to Him and desire to be more like Him. The first chapter covers "Discovering Christ-like Joy" and the final chapter is "Christlike Love." Other chapters include lessons on integrity, self-control, humility, and forgiveness. Each lesson also introduces an unreached people group to help you understand the peoples of our world. Ask your parent or home school teacher to check it out at ***www.DeeperRoots.com*** where they can order FREE pdf sample pages from the teacher's guide.

(Some 10th graders will enjoy this study after completing the first three studies)

231DHHSTG Home School (Teacher's Guide)...$28.95

232DHHSSW Home School (Student Workbook) ...$19.95

Rooted & Grounded, A Guide for Spiritual Growth
Suitable for 10th or 11th or 12th Grade
Howard & Bonnie Lisech and Jan Harris, Deeper Roots Publications

Rooted and Grounded can be used for one or possibly two years of Home School high school Bible classes. Encouragement for Christian living is presented in an appealing and easy-to-use format. Each of the 27 lessons focuses on an important spiritual principle. In addition to essential principles for success in a student's spiritual life, you are introduced to world missions as you move from biblical ***knowledge*** to spiritual ***application*** while completing these studies. Every lesson begins with an unreached people group profile that features beautiful pencil sketches by artist Julie Bosacker. Ask your parent or home school teacher to check it out at ***www.DeeperRoots.com*** where they can order FREE pdf sample pages from the teacher's guide.

101RGTG Teacher's Guide...$39.50

102RGSW Student's Workbook...$23.95

103RGTEST Unit Tests & Answer Keys ...$3.95

A Glimpse of God's Majesty

Suitable for 11th or12th Grade

Howard & Bonnie Lisech and Jan Harris, Deeper Roots Publications